Lee —

Best of Success!

Thanks for a

Great Week!

Champion "U"
2005

Tom Hopkins'

LOW PROFILE SELLING

Act Like a Lamb. Sell Like a Lion.

NOTE TO OUR READERS: In Chapter 6, we teach the power of words. In it, we recommend that you replace words you say now that may generate fear in your prospects with more powerful, positive words and phrases. Since most of our readers will require study time to learn the new terms, we've left the old terms in some areas to enhance the comprehension of the concepts.

Published by Tom Hopkins International, Inc.
7531 East Second Street
Scottsdale, Arizona, USA 85251
(800) 528-0446 (480) 949-0786 Fax (480) 949-1590
Web site: http://www.tomhopkins.com
E-mail: th@tomhopkins.com

20 19 18 17 16 15 14

ISBN #0-938636-29-4

Portions of this book have appeared as copyrighted cassette recordings and video tape.

DEDICATION

It is with great appreciation that I dedicate this book to Judy Slack. Her creativity, hard work, and commitment to me and Tom Hopkins International have enabled us to become leaders in the field of sales training. Judy has been an integral part of our video, audio, and book publications for over twenty years. If there were to be an unsung hero in our company, it would be Judy Slack.

CONTENTS

INTRODUCTION

My first book, "How to Master the Art of Selling," has become a text-book for professional selling over the years. In fact, it has sold over a million copies. In it, we take a very in-depth look at all phases of the selling process.

In my seminars, video and audio tapes, I teach that the process of making a sale consists of seven steps. They are as follows: Prospecting, Original Contact, Qualification, Presentation or Demonstration, Handling Objections, Closing and Getting Referrals.

Our studies have shown that most career salespeople work to become fairly proficient in each of the seven areas. We have discovered, though, that four of the seven areas seem to carry more weight when it comes to actual income generated. So, even though it is necessary to master all seven steps of selling, our focus in this book will be directed to those four key areas: original contact, qualification, objections and closing, and how questioning techniques interact with all of those four areas.

Each of these topics is taught and demonstrated in a certain style. It is a style I suggest you consider adopting if you truly have the desire to become successful in your selling career.

The style you apply to each step of the selling cycle is critical to success in any sales career. You see, salesmanship is more than the words you say. It is how you deliver those words. In selling, we all know that your words must be great but if your style is wrong, your sales can suffer tremendously. If you have watched my video role plays you know my approach is very laid back and soft.

So, as we cover our four topics, we will concentrate on style. I will also try to convince you that you need to become a student of selling --to make selling and the study of selling your hobby.

To become truly successful in this business, you need to watch and study others in selling situations of all kinds. Open your mind to the many selling situations around you — in which you are not the salesperson — and you'll be amazed at how much you can learn.

We are all barraged with sales strategies every day. Our loved ones sell us on ideas every day. Politicians try to sell us on voting for them. Girl Scouts sell millions of cookies every spring. Our co-workers sell us on where to go for lunch. Once there, the waiter or waitress sells us on the special of the day. The list is endless.

Every one of us is selling, or being sold, every minute of every day. We are bombarded by advertising from the time we awaken until we go to sleep. It starts on the radio when the alarm goes off each morning. The average American sees nearly one hundred ads on television during daily viewing. ONE HUNDRED ADS!

Billboards line the roads to and from work or shopping. Magazines and newspapers are loaded with products and services we are being told to buy. After all, written advertising is nothing more than salesmanship in print. We are surrounded by people wanting to get our attention, interest and desire for their product.

Begin today to notice what does get your attention in these "selling situations." Then ask yourself why you noticed them or why you felt the way you did about the product. What works on you and what doesn't? What grabs you? What turns you off?

The key is, don't just be turned on or off. Ask yourself why. Why did that person or that ad affect me that way? What pictures did it create in my mind? What emotions did it stir? Were they positive or negative?

The more answers you come up with, the more sensitive you will become to the words and actions that can make or break sales. Then, consider how you can use the same style, words, and emotions that worked on you to sell others your product or service. Please note, once you begin analyzing selling situations, you'll also learn words, phrases and emotions to avoid — those that turned you off. That can be just as valuable a lesson.

I have been a student of selling for over 25 years, and I can honestly say that more people are talked out of buying each day than are talked into a sale. If you doubt that, read further in this book. Then watch salespeople and customers in sales situations and judge for yourself.

I hope as you watch and listen to others, you will do so with a spirit of learning and use what you see and hear to get better at selling, and to help others understand what you have learned.

Selling is a wonderful love/hate relationship that can take you on an emotional roller-coaster ride. You have to love the people who get into sales because they make a statement about themselves. They are willing to put themselves on the line each day and expose their egos to more rejection than a non-salesperson gets in a month in order to get more from life. That's why I love salespeople. I just wish I could get more of them to do what you are doing now — to read, study, and practice how to improve their selling skills.

Too many salespeople make their first few sales on personality and enthusiasm and think they are "naturals" at it. They don't believe they need any training. Then comes a downturn in the economy, or the competition comes out with a better product, and suddenly they're not making sales any more. Then, the salesperson's personality isn't quite as bubbly and their enthusiasm is waning. They don't know what happened or how it happened, but they're in a frightening downward spiral. Soon they go back to their old jobs, bitter about their failed selling "career." The sad truth that many of them never understand is that they really never were in selling because they never learned how to sell.

If you have ever been to one of my seminars, you know I say there is no such thing as a natural born salesperson. There are no naturals at selling, including me.

My first six months in sales were devastating. Many things happened during that time that seem funny to me today, but believe me, I wasn't laughing at the time. I did more squirming than laughing in those days.

It's an interesting thing about laughter and happiness. If you look for them, they're always within reach. Through all my early trials and tribulations I learned that happiness belongs in the present, not in the future "when I am successful." If you postpone happiness and laughter, there is a good chance you will also postpone your success. Decide to be happy now. Make the pursuit of laughter and happiness one of your favorite pastimes, and life will hold many rewards for you.

This sounds idealistic, doesn't it? It isn't, but it can often be hard advice to follow especially when you are 19 years old, newly married with a baby on the way, and averaging a whopping $42 a month during your first six months.

I was beside myself with worry. I was getting as little sleep as I was getting positive results in my selling career. I was a very unhappy young man with a tender ego. Do you think I was negative, depressed, and ready to give up selling? You bet I was. The problem was I had quit college after 90 days, and I didn't want to quit sales too. I was afraid to consider myself a quitter. I had something to prove to all those people who didn't think I'd ever amount to anything, especially my father.

You see, after quitting college, my father had a long talk with me about my future. It ended with him telling me that he and my mother would always love me even though I would never amount to anything.

Month after month, it began to look as if he was right. The way I figured it, I had only two choices. Either I needed to learn what I was doing wrong and correct it, or give up my dreams and take a salaried job with none of the benefits of the selling profession. I had to take action fast or the money pressures would dictate the course my life would take. I don't know about you, but I hate anything being forced on me, so I took action. I took control of my own life.

One day, just about the time I came to this "take action" realization, I glanced out the window and saw a sleek sports car pull into the parking lot. I watched as an impeccably dressed young man stepped out of it and headed for our door. He had such an air of success about him that it fascinated me. I went to the front desk, introduced myself to him and asked what he did. With an aura of confidence I had never seen in a salesperson before, he said that he was in sales.

"How are you doing?" I questioned.

"Very well, I'll probably earn $25,000 this year." Remember, this was in the early 1960's, and then, $25,000 was a lot of money.

"How do you do it?" I again questioned, somewhat awestruck.

"I learned how to sell," was his reply.

I went on to tell him that I was thinking of leaving sales because I felt it wasn't for me.

He carefully listened to my discouraged words and then said, "Have you ever heard of J. Douglas Edwards?"

"No."

"He's the master of selling skills."

"Great! But what's that to me?"

"He will teach you everything you need to say and do. If you apply the knowledge he gives you, you can make it big in sales."

"That's what I need." I said.

Have you ever heard a friend or acquaintance mention something and suddenly you know you'd never be the same again? Well, this gentleman had ignited a fire within me. You see, gaining more knowledge about the art of selling was more than something I needed, it was something I wanted. I was already emotionally involved.

At the time, the company I worked for had a training program that went something like this: "Hang in there." I'm sure you'll agree it wasn't too helpful.

That well-dressed young man sat down with me and in the next 30 minutes, persuaded me to attend the Edwards' training program. It cost me $150 to attend. That was not only a lot of money at that point in my not-so-illustrious sales career, it was everything I had. I invested everything in my future. I took the training and met the man who was to become my mentor — J. Douglas Edwards. He was fantastic. He made me realize there was so much to learn about selling. He also made the wild claim that salespeople were taught to be great. They were not born that way. Who would have guessed you could learn to sell? Back then, everyone I spoke with thought if you had the gift of gab, which they said I had, you could make it big in sales.

About that "gift" of gab, if you think you have it, or if someone has said you do, please realize right now that it's not a gift. When I first began my sales career, I could talk a mile a minute and people seemed to like me, but I wasn't making any sales.

So, I decided right then to get as much as possible from that course. I took notes like mad. I studied night and day to internalize what Mr. Edwards taught. Once I started putting it to use, I started making sales. I couldn't believe it.

Over the next few years, I set many sales records and went on to become one of the top real estate salespeople in the United States. Some of the records I set were pretty incredible and still stand today, but it was only because I had the knowledge and was willing to continually study and work to get better.

I won all kinds of trophies and awards and was asked to speak to large groups of salespeople. I had gone from chump to champ in a relatively short time thanks to that sales training from Mr. Edwards. He really opened my eyes to the fact that selling is a learned skill and now I hope to open your eyes.

Hopefully, you're ready for a positive change in your selling career. Let me give you a little warning, though: It will take some work on your part. There were also several other people from my office who attended that sales training program many years ago. They obviously saw the training differently than I did, because only a couple of them did what I did — study, practice, and use the material — and went on to become really good at selling. Most of the group only made a half-hearted attempt at learning and using the material. And, guess what? They didn't get much out of it. Soon, many of them were out of selling and back at their old jobs. This still totally amazes me. Here was this incredible material on which to lay a foundation of a phenomenal career and they weren't taking advantage of it. Why wasn't it as obvious to them as it was to me? I think the answer is that they just couldn't get it through their heads that selling was a learned skill.

I had people tell me, over and over, how I was lucky that I had some natural abilities. Believe me, no one knows better than I how untrue that statement is. I learned the hard way that selling is a learned skill, just like reading and writing, and the more you work at it the better you become.

I've shared this story with you because I'm trying to convince you that you're on the right track in your quest for knowledge of selling skills. I also want you to know that I can empathize with anyone who is broke or off to a slow start in selling. I will be making a case throughout this whole book on the value of your continued education in selling and in the study of human emotion.

As salespeople, we are professional problem-solvers. We help others get what they want and get paid to do it. So, let's give up being incompetent and unprepared. Let's become part of the solution for our customers and not part of the problem.

CHAPTER 1
LAMB OR LION? YOUR CHOICE.

To give you an understanding of how our philosophy **"Act Like A Lamb, Sell Like A Lion"** works, just imagine this: Imagine yourself as a wandering customer lost in the jungle of sales. You hunt and hunt for the product or service that will be the most beneficial to you. Just when you think you have found the product or service that's just right, out of the brush steps a lion. The lion's roar turns you off and frightens you. Your needs can't be heard over the lion's intimidating roar. He gives chase with overbearing aggressiveness and you run away before you ever discover if the lion could have guided you in your hunt. The lion made you feel like you were the prey rather than the hunter.

Next, you come across a friendly lamb, grazing in the high grasses beside your path. As you pass, the lamb notices your confusion and asks if you need help. The lamb listens as you tell of your hunt for the right product or service, gently offering advice along the way. Before you know it, you have stopped wandering, you feel good because you have discovered for yourself (with just a little lamb-like help) the most beneficial offering, and now you naturally turn to the lamb for advice on how you can own the offering.

You see, unlike the lion that practiced the fear and power-struggle method of sales, the lamb demonstrated genuine concern for you, the customer. This type of sales is called low profile selling.

Low profile selling can be a difficult concept to grasp because most people think that selling means being loud, aggressive, and pushy—the

1

lion approach. Many people in selling reject the idea of sales training for just that reason. They feel someone is going to try to make them aggressive and loud, like the class bully, and teach them all sorts of obnoxious traits. This is a frightening thought for most people, especially women.

If it is not necessary for the Champion salesman to exhibit a "king of the jungle" mentality in sales, it is certainly true that the professional saleswoman can be soft and feminine (the lamb approach) while practicing the art of successful sales.

In fact many salespeople, especially women, start out successfully in sales with a quiet, lamb-like approach. Unfortunately, most of them don't understand that their approach is one of the major reasons for their success. When they hit a slump or set a goal for higher sales, they tend to become more aggressive about making sales and may lose their natural lamb-like advantage.

Your style and sales strategy should be deliberately flexible to meet the customer's needs, not just to fulfill your own. It is my belief that most people in sales are polite and considerate and would like to stay that way, so where did this negative image of a salesperson as a loud-mouthed monster come from?

Unfortunately, I think much of the salesperson's negative image has come from the movies and television. Stamped on the minds of millions of viewers is a negative picture the typical salesperson. This person is usually portrayed as a conniving loud-mouthed idiot with no ethics, wearing a plaid coat with a wide paisley tie or a double-knit polyester suit. Or, they are shown too well-dressed and slick. The main goal of this salesperson is to cheat some poor widow out of her life savings. Well, there you have it. It's no wonder there's such a negative image of us in the world. Let this be a perfect example for you to choose your educators carefully. Don't depend on what you see on television, in the movies or in the newspapers to be the sum total of your educational experience, or you will be doing yourself and your customers a disservice.

With that negative image in mind, who would want to identify with this poor image of the typical salesperson? No one. So let's change this image by improving our selling skills. Today's highly sophisticated consumers require and expect a high degree of professionalism in salespeople. The true Champions recognize and fulfill this need.

In the next few chapters I hope to convince you, with my more than 25 years of selling experience, that true professional selling is just the opposite of how most of the world views it. If you, as a salesperson or small businessperson, will strive to comprehend and apply the material in this book, you can avoid the tragedy experienced by so many people who are naive to the benefits of acquiring professional sales skills.

Small Business Failures -- The American Tragedy

Let's take a look at the statistics that reflect the failure rate of small businesses. We live in an era of statistics. There seem to be statistics for just about everything. Among those statistics are births and deaths. I'm not talking here about people, but of the businesses they own and operate. The mortality rate for businesses is increasing at an alarming rate.

One of the worst and most unnecessary statistics is that over 90% of new businesses in the U.S. fail in their first five years. It is difficult for me to imagine the extent of the hopes and dreams that have crumbled under the heavy burden of debt, mismanagement, or inadequate education. Those entrepreneurs courageous enough to fight the odds and begin their own businesses certainly deserve better.

Oftentimes success was there for the taking, if only they had known where to look—toward others in their field who had experienced what they were going through and could have shared their formulas for success (or at least how to avoid failure).

All of these businesses shared common aspirations. They all sold a product or service to the public, or to other businesses. They all started with high hopes, much hard work and in many cases a shortage of capital. I believe most set out to do everything right, like getting a lawyer to set up the corporation or partnership. Then they sought accounting help and excitedly opened for business, thinking they were ready to have the world beat a path to their door. They believed this would happen because of their extensive business plans, or because their product or service was so good, or even because they were committed to the success of their new business. However, they soon got a strong dose of reality when they were not getting enough customers, and most of the customers they did get were "lookers" or "be-backs." How many of these entrepreneurs do you think had any sales and marketing experience? One out of ten maybe? The simple fact is that the biggest deficit many of those entrepreneurs faced was not in cash flow, or desire, or even hard work, but rather a deficit in the knowledge of selling and marketing skills. It's a shame that so many volumes have been written and recorded on sales and marketing, yet they still remain unread and unheard. This lack of education can trigger so much havoc in people's lives. After all, that's what we are really speaking of, isn't it? It's not about profit and loss of a business: It's about the lives those businesses support.

How many businesses today, that are not showing the kind of profits their owners or managers would like, could use this knowledge? I think you'd be hard-pressed to find one that can't. So why don't they take advantage of that knowledge? They don't because they are all too often unaware of its existence. Most people in the business of business just don't know that there is an enormous amount of valuable and easy-to-use information available to help them solve their business problems. Or, they are so busy wearing all the hats that come with running a business that they don't make time to learn.

You should consider yourself lucky, if not just plain smart. You are already one step ahead of the game. You have embarked on what should now become a life-long educational journey that will lead you to making wise business decisions. You see, education doesn't stop after high school or college, or after you leave the classroom. It stops only when you close your mind to knowledge, when you refuse to learn from your experiences, when you say, "NO" to continued growth and potential success.

Low Profile Selling

Low profile selling may be a difficult concept to grasp, because most people believe that to sell anything you have to be aggressive and pushy. That negative association most people have of a bulldozing salesperson, in reality, wouldn't last long in today's market.

The "old timer" who has refused to keep up with the demands of today's sophisticated customer, or the "new kid on the block" who thinks it is his way or the highway, may still believe that those strong-arm tactics work, (if they ever did). However, those types of salespeople and their course greatly differs from that of the successful professional. Champion salespeople have learned the power of low profile selling—low pressure/high powered sales techniques.

Major corporations spend millions each year training and retraining their sales forces, yet even executives who leave these major corporations to go into business for themselves often overlook the importance of professional selling skills. Let me say this: How do you think those companies became major corporations in the first place?

One of the main benefits of sales training is that you can increase your sales without increasing overhead. For the business owner, you don't have to hire more salespeople to get more sales. Simply increase the skills of those salespeople you already have. Sales training is one of the least expensive ways a company or an individual can increase their bottom line. It's a fascinating process and a very profitable one. All the costs remain constant as your sales ratios climb. But what about the individual salesperson?

The same applies to the individual salesperson. If you are a salesperson wanting to increase your income, please understand that you don't have to devote more hours to selling to increase your sales, just increase your selling skills instead. You will be closing more sales in the same amount of time. You see, if you want to make more money, you have two choices—you can try to sell to more customers, or you can get better at selling. Since there are only so many customers you can see before you reach saturation and only so much time in which you can sell, I suggest the latter. Work smarter, not harder. Seeing too many customers will limit your ability to give each and every one of them the good service they deserve. Since service is the essence of professional sales, isn't it wise to get better at serving those customers you sell thus building a strong base of good customers?

I hope we can agree that selling has a bad name with many people because high pressure and high-handedness are identified with high production. This is why people are dubious when I speak of low-profile and high-income selling. How can low-profile selling get the job done? That is what the rest of this book is about. **Quiet power**.

Focus on the Prospect

I think it is important to note that the prospect is always the "Star" in any selling situation, but guess who controls the spotlight? You guessed it. The well-trained salesperson remains in control. The truly professional salesperson steps out of the spotlight and allows the one parting with the money to take the bows for making a wise decision. It is your job to make your prospect look good, after all, there are many other available spotlight specialists waiting offstage to take your place. Be there to provide information, help rationalize their misgivings, and encourage them to overcome fear and procrastination. Be interested, not interesting. You can only be successful at this by listening, and you can't be listening if you are doing all the talking—like the lion. Too often, lions roar just to hear themselves roar. That's exactly the image we are trying to get away from in professional selling. The image we are trying to achieve is the dignity and respect due the "king of the jungle" but presented with a lamb-like, inoffensive personality.

Act like a lamb and let your customer talk. This is where 90% of salespeople make their mistake. Thinking it necessary for the salesperson to maintain an endless stream of conversation is perhaps the most misunderstood aspect of selling. I've been trying to get this point across to salespeople and managers for over 20 years.

It is always wiser to choose what you say than to say what you choose. When necessary, take a few moments to think about what it is you really want to say, and how you can best say it. It is perfectly acceptable to have a break in the conversation if it shows you are carefully considering what has just been said. This will make your customers feel as if what they have to say is important. So listen. Listen to what they have to say, pausing when necessary to allow everyone to analyze the information, then respond with thoughtful consideration to their concerns. The key word is to listen. Now you're getting it, **ACT LIKE A LAMB, SELL LIKE A LION**.

Most salespeople think they should be Mr. or Ms. Personality, and show off as they throw around all kinds of brilliant knowledge and meaningful advice. This is probably the biggest destroyer of sales. Why? Because they haven't learned to shut up and listen. Did you ever wonder that there just might be a good reason, in the greater scheme of things, that we have two ears and only one mouth. I believe the old saying that our Creator intended us to listen at least twice as much as we talk. As a salesperson you exist for only one reason, to serve your customer. To do that, you have to find out how you can serve them. You should be gaining as much information as possible about what they want or think they want. Hopefully, you will find the value of acting like a lamb and holding your tongue when necessary, so you yourself are not a distraction or a nuisance in the selling process.

Manners and respect should be your number one personal focus. Strive to be polite and low key. Avoid any mannerisms that could break the prospect's train of thought. You don't want them focusing on the pen you constantly roll between your fingers, or the earlobe you pull when you are nervous or your bad habit of running your fingers through your hair or touching your chin or nose.

Your wardrobe should be appropriate for your customer base. You don't want to be over-dressed or under-dressed. For example, if you are selling farming equipment to the local landowner, don't wear your custom-tailored Italian silk suit—casual slacks or jeans and a nice shirt would probably put your customers more at ease. However, a boardroom full of executives are not too likely to be impressed with that attire. This would be the time for more businesslike attire. You should look and act professionally, but don't outshine the prospect. Remember, the prospect is the star of the show.

It is necessary for you to realize that every little detail in selling is important. The decision to buy, or not to buy, can hang on very small actions or words, as well as appearances. The more you leave to chance, the more chance you leave that your income will be less than anticipated. Work on ways to improve. Record yourself during a sales presentation. Examine your speech habits. Keep what is positive for sales, throw out what is unproductive. Look at yourself when you think you are dressed as a pro. Can you make changes for the better? If so, go to work. You are responsible for creating your own positive first impression. The more professionally you conduct yourself, the more your sales will go up. It's your choice.

Seven Steps of Successful Selling

When I teach new salespeople the basics of selling, I can only go so far because there is so much to learn. I can't get too involved for fear of making students self-conscious of their every move and word. For new salespeople, too much self analysis could be destructive to their egos. We all know you get enough ego knocks as new salespeople anyway. We save their egos until they have survived at least six months in the field and are ready for more advanced training. Then they learn the more in-depth information at my three day advanced sales training academies. The average income of the students at my advanced courses is over $60,000 per year. Over 20% of the attendees usually earn over $100,000 a year, so they're big enough to allow their egos to tolerate some bruising in the name of a positive learning experience.

In three days we cover the whole sales cycle in much more detail, so that even less is left to chance.

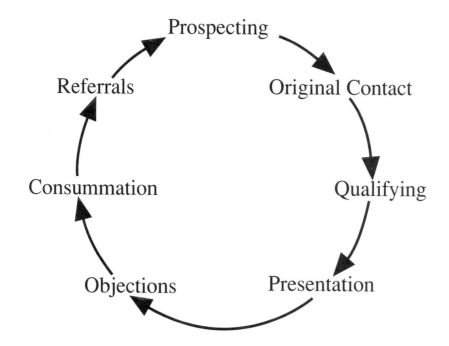

The seven steps we teach in the selling cycle are:

1. Prospecting: covers non-referral and telephone
2. Making an original contact
3. Qualification
4. Presentation
5. Handling objections
6. Consummation (commonly known as closing the sale)
7. Getting referrals

I'm sure you will agree that the level of competence you establish in each of these steps will determine how successful you are overall, and it will have a direct link to your income. Unfortunately, many salespeople have not come to this realization. They try to take shortcuts, and the shortcuts usually bypass one or more of the four critical steps: original contact, qualification, handling objections, or closing the sale. This is why we have chosen to focus our attention on these four key areas in particular.

It has been my experience that many salespeople will avoid admitting and working on the weakest areas in their sales technique. It's human nature not to want to face up to or admit our faults and weaknesses. The problem is, if you are weak at any one of these, then your income drops accordingly.

Maybe the problem is that you can't distinguish your strengths from your weaknesses. If this is the case, you will find it helpful to fill out a sales evaluation that will pinpoint your sales aptitude. We have developed a sales skill evaluation tool with Dr. Gregory Lousig-Nont, an industrial psychologist who has studied salespeople and their skills for over five years. The $ales $uccess Profile was developed after analysis of the skill levels of over 350,000 salespeople. On the basis of this study, we now know the areas critical to any selling career. We know the difference in skill level of a salesperson earning $25,000 per year and a sales professional who earns around $100,000 per year. We have documented the specific areas of sales in which those high income earners excel. Keep reading and you will find that this book will help you to focus on four of the selling skills at which our top income-earners excel: original contact, qualification, handling objections, and closing the sale. It will show you how you can turn them into your strengths.

Let me illustrate my point by looking at another type of professional—the professional athlete. Everybody has heard of Jack Nicklaus, probably one of the world's greatest golfers. If Jack didn't know how to use all of his golf clubs well, which one do you think he could be poor at using and still have the career he has? The answer is none. He needs to know every club in his bag and be competent with each one. At his level of competition, any club that he is not competent with would have a tremendous negative affect on his income.

It's like that in sales, too. If you are weak in qualifying, you'll be spending much of your valuable selling time talking with people who are not qualified to own your product or service. In selling, determining your weak areas isn't quite as easy as it is in golf because the steps to selling are interrelated.

In golf, if you hit poorly with a 7-iron, you can go out and practice your skill with that club alone. In selling, giving a poor presentation could result from several weak skill areas: (1) You could just be a poor presenter. (2) You could be a poor qualifier and present the wrong product or service. (3) You could be weak in original contact and have turned off a highly qualified prospect.

Since there are more subtleties to selling than in golf, you need to constantly diagnose your abilities. If you have challenges with your presentations, try changing them a bit. If that doesn't work, you might consider qualifying your prospects more thoroughly before preparing a presentation. If that doesn't work, develop more personal communication skills and learn more ways to develop rapport with your clients.

There are any number of minor changes you can make to improve your success at presenting. The important thing is to try them one at a time until you find what works. Then, develop that skill to an art. Master it and your income will soar.

It works that way with the tools of any profession, weak skills equal weak results. You can't be spectacular in handling objections yet be a wishy-washy closer and expect top results. This is the reason for continued training. We have found that the big income earners are especially eager to improve on their weaknesses!

So, at my three-day, high-intensity programs, we cover in great detail every one of these steps without regard to feelings or egos, especially on the subject of closing the sale. As beginners, I have students memorize closes. In the advanced course, I have them writing their own. The result is a calm enthusiasm and self-confidence that does not need to be expressed in excess talk or wild actions.

Listen and Sell with CALM Enthusiasm

What about that concept, calm enthusiasm? Wouldn't you agree, most people don't think of a correlation between calm and enthusiasm?

Let's take a closer look. Is there a relationship between the two? Is there such a thing as too much of a good thing, too much enthusiasm? I think so. I always caution my students not to overflow with enthusiasm. You will probably only make a mess of everything. Instead, keep your cup full of enthusiasm, but don't let it slop over where it can damage all your hard work. Henry Ford once said:

> "You can do anything if you have enthusiasm.
> Enthusiasm is the yeast that makes your hopes
> rise to the stars. Enthusiasm is the spark
> in your eye, the swing in your gait, the grip
> of your hand, the irresistible surge of your
> will and your energy to execute your ideas.
> Enthusiasts are fighters, they have fortitude,
> they have staying qualities. Enthusiasm is at
> the bottom of all progress! With it, there is
> accomplishment. Without it, there are only
> alibis."

What a wonderful truism. Why not put enthusiasm behind all your efforts, instead of expecting it to cover up what could be a lack of preparation and knowledge on your part. Think of it this way, when your prospects leave you, what do you want them to take with them? Your enthusiasm, or ownership of what you are offering?

So, the focus of this whole book is **quiet power**. Why is quiet good? Well, let's look at what happens when you are doing the majority of the talking. Remind yourself of these facts when you are tempted to make communication a one-way street. Repeat them to yourself. When I talk too much:

1. I am not learning about the customer or customer's needs.
2. I will not hear buying clues or concern.
3. I may be raising concerns the prospect might not have had.
4. I shift their attention and from interest in my offering to me.
5. I give them more opportunity to disagree with me or distrust one of my statements.
6. I take center stage away from the customer.
7. I can't think ahead.
8. I can't guide the conversation.
9. I cannot convince the customer of the best decision for them.

I am sure we could add a lot more to this list, however, I think you get the idea. Most of us don't think we talk too much during the sale, but if you could listen to as many sales presentations as I have over 25 years of teaching, selling, and sales management, you would develop a keen ear for how much talking is needed.

To develop your ear I would suggest two simple exercises:

1. Listen to salespeople selling others or trying to sell you and pay attention to what their words are doing. Are their words painting positive mental pictures or negative? Are they saying anything that could raise a new objection to their product or service in your mind? Are all the words necessary? Are they asking questions and then listening carefully to the answers? Are they moving forward with questions, or are they getting off course talking about features and benefits the customer has not expressed a need for? Are they making the customer the star or are they hogging the spotlight?

2. If you make a recording of yourself with a customer, you may be shocked at the amount of chatter you can cut out. What is the quality of the questions you ask? Are they information-gathering questions to help you move forward with your sale, or are they just questions you are asking to fill a sound void? Questions don't mean much unless the answers are helping you get the information to help you serve your customer better and keep the sales momentum going.

Be a Student of Selling

I can't encourage you strongly enough to work at being a student of selling. In the dictionary, the word study comes before the word success, and it should be that way in your program for sales success. Look at how much you would lose if everything were handed to you on a silver platter. One of the biggest senses of loss you would experience would be that of achievement, the personal reward felt when you achieve success through your own hard work and perseverance. Study the art, science, and skills of professional selling. As I mentioned before, watch other people in sales. What do they do that could help you? What do they do that you want to avoid? Pay close attention to the world around you. Wonder about things. When you are not in front of a customer, get near someone who is. Don't just sit around.

As you study different salespeople, grade them on how you think they did, but keep it to yourself. You might grade them on these areas:

1. Good questions that give informative feedback
2. Unnecessary talk
3. Raising objections
4. Good listening
5. Taking notes
6. Negative words or word pictures
7. Making the customer the star by involving them in the presentation
8. Moving forward smoothly
9. Offensive statements, if any

10. Habit words like "You know." or "You know what I mean?"
11. Nervous habits like hair flipping, pen twirling, adjusting clothing, jewelry, sniffling or cracking knuckles
12. Making just enough eye contact
13. Having a pleasing deportment and posture
14. Whether they are calm and professional

You might be asking yourself why these things are important. Once you start taking notice of them, I believe you will see just how weak most sales efforts are. You will actually hear people being talked out of buying — turned off by unknowing salespeople. Poor selling techniques will become obvious to you.

A well-trained professional with good skills makes it look so easy when helping the customer, that many people would refer to this person as a "natural." I'm sure you have heard, "Oh, they're just a natural at selling." Don't kid yourself. The professional salesperson is very much in tune with the customer and follows each step of the selling sequence carefully. They have learned not to take short cuts. The most important thing of all—they put all their knowledge to work by doing.

The reason it is so important to see and hear this is so you become a believer in these skills, and that you can become a "natural" also. Anyone who can read, re-read, study this book, and then follow its teaching will greatly increase the level of service they provide to their customers. When you increase customer service, you raise the standard of living for both you and your prospects. This is something each of us desires, isn't it?

Why Silence is Golden

As you become a student of low profile selling, you will watch and listen to yourself and others more carefully. It may be helpful to first practice your listening skills when you are not in a selling situation. Acquaint yourself with what good listening really "sounds" like. It should sound like the voice of others, not yours. The phrase, "Putting your foot in your mouth" will gain new meaning for you. Remember, you can't put your foot in your mouth if it's closed. So close it, and listen more. If you have a choice, be an introvert not an extrovert. Be interested because you only learn when you are listening. If you have to choose, choose to talk too little. Don't seek attention, give attention. Keep the ego in check.

The truth is, most salespeople are somewhere in the middle. My ideal salesperson would possess qualities like these:

* Unafraid with an air of quiet calm
* Great presence but always modest
* Lets actions do the talking
* Is willing to be judged by results
* Ego does not need to be center stage

I have found it is easier to train a shy, quiet person to ask good questions, listen, and take notes, than it is to make a very talkative person attentive enough to ask and listen to the answers. Silence seems to scare some people. It takes a real effort to stop talking and listen, especially if you have a strong mental image of a salesperson with the "gift of gab." It's unfortunate, but many sales careers have been cut short or ruined by new people taking on this type of persona, filling every moment with unnecessary talk.

As we move through this book, we will try to expose and overcome any desire on your part to dominate your customers. As you come to understand your sales role, it will get much easier.

CHAPTER 2
TAKE A CLUE FROM JEOPARDY®, ASK THE RIGHT QUESTION AND YOU WIN

The beginning of learning is curiosity. When we are curious, we ask questions. We investigate. We learn. Your prospects may already be curious about your product or service. If so, then, you must follow their lead and be curious about why they have this interest. Advertising and other promotions are designed specifically to create curiosity in those people who may not already know about your product or service. The best way to learn and satisfy our curiosity is to ask questions. It's that way with every aspect of learning.

Let's use the medical profession as an example. What do doctors do when you come in? They start asking questions. They ask you to describe what you're feeling -- what your current situation is. They use good questioning techniques, along with diagnostic equipment to gather more information. Once they have a clear picture of your symptoms, they ask yes/no questions to narrow down the choice of illnesses you might have and potential treatments. Their number one goal is to give you what's best for you and help you enjoy the benefits of good health.

Your job as a salesperson can easily compare to this example. Your goal should be helping your customers enjoy the benefits of your offering. You can best reach that goal through the use of effective questions. Your diagnostic equipment can be as simple as a pad of paper, measuring tape, or a calculator. It can even be as complex as a computer, or even your own experiences and memory stored in your brain. Lastly, questions eliminate what the prospect doesn't need and zero-in on the product or service that will solve the customer's problem or create an opportunity for them. The customized question form we mentioned earlier will ensure you get all the information you need to give the best possible service.

The average salesperson has a fantasy in which they think they should be able to simply present the wonderful features of their product or service and the customer will automatically see its worth, write a check and take it home. That would be fine if customer's perceptions were always created through a logical analysis of the product, and you were a lucky enough salesperson to represent the best of all products. We all know, this is certainly not how it happens in reality.

In reality, buying decisions are based on past experiences, the experiences of others, advertising, gut feelings, and hundreds of other factors that vary from client to client. None of which can be controlled by the salesperson. However, salespeople do need to acquire just that kind of background information before they can determine the best approach and the best product or service to present to the customer. The best way to do this, if not the only way, is to ask plenty of questions to get the customer talking about their needs, wants and perceptions of your product or service.

As an example, let's consider a couple in their 60's who are in your store, looking at VCR's. They've never owned one before and know little about electronics. Their need for a VCR is simply to play video tapes of the grandchildren who live a thousand miles away. They may want the VCR also so they can rent movies rather than going out to the theater. However, they may view today's high technology products with skepticism and a certain degree of confusion. The salesperson's goal with this couple should be to demonstrate the simplest machine they have to offer and get them emotionally involved in the enjoyment they'll receive in watching the grandchildren's tapes any time they want. The salesperson should put low emphasis on all of the other wonderful features of the machine. These people don't care if it can be programmed to record an event at 3:00 AM in the year 2050. The wise salesperson will understand that the technical knowledge he or she is so proud of is inappropriate here. Such talk might intimidate these buyers and make them want to postpone making a decision.

One of the most important points I teach salespeople is to get themselves out of the way in every selling situation. What seems easy and even exciting to them about the product or service may be of absolutely no interest to the prospect or difficult for them to understand. The salesperson should always strive to put themselves in the shoes of the customer. <u>Never attempt to have them walk in your shoes</u>.

So, how does the salesperson learn just what each buyer's situation is? By asking questions and encouraging the couple to talk about why they have an interest in a VCR. With proper questions, the salesperson will learn that this is their first VCR purchase and that they may be a bit afraid of making a decision on something outside their usual realm of purchases. The emotions of the buyer should always be considered ahead of the logic in making the investment. Logic does come into play, but usually it's used to defend an emotional purchase.

So what other human elements besides logic and need will determine what the customer perceives to be the best? The Champion salesperson recognizes that the most potent force is perception, and then appeals to that force. We may have the best product for our customer, not only is it more durable and less costly, it also has features no other model has. We can determine that our prospect needs our product's exclusive features. That's the reality, but what is the truth? The truth is that the prospects will not buy your superior product unless they believe all the things you tell them are true. How do you get them to believe what you know is true?

Don't Tell, Ask

How do you get prospects to believe what you know is true? Well, you can **tell** them. You can dazzle them with all kinds of fancy graphs and numbers and force the facts down their throats. You can **tell** them how incorrect their thinking is because they simply won't admit the truth of your statements. If you handle your presentation that way, it's highly likely they'll still not be convinced. That's because you have **told** them.

You have not appealed to the customers' emotions, except to turn them off with your attitude.

There is another way to get your customers to believe what you say. Don't you say it--get them to say it. By this, I don't mean getting them in a choke hold until they holler "uncle." Remember, the theme of this book is low profile. The truth of the matter is if you say it, they tend to doubt it. After all, it's your job to say great things about your product or service in order to close the sale. But, if they say something about your product or service, they must believe it. Your job is to ask the right questions that encourage them to say the same thing you would otherwise be telling them. This way, the customers get the pleasure of discovering for themselves all the wonderful benefits your product or service has to offer.

Let's say you know that a certain feature of your product or service has saved all of your other customers three minutes of time in a rather lengthy process. Instead of saying, "This feature saves you three minutes of time in the process," you should ask, "How do you think this feature would benefit you?" If you've demonstrated your product effectively, it should be obvious to them to answer, "It'll save a good bit of time during the overall process." They've just said it. They must believe it.

By getting your customers emotionally involved in your product or service, I don't mean you should try to destroy their belief in the product or service they are now using. Some trainers actually teach doing this, but I believe this is dangerous and unnecessary. You have no way of knowing how strongly your customers believe in what they have been using. Such a tactic could cause them to become defensive, creating a barrier you'll have to work hard to overcome. They may be proud of having made the original purchase and in destroying what they believed to be true about the past, you are causing them to admit they made a mistake or that they could have made a wiser decision. Either way, they lose face. You have now created an emotional involvement ;with your customer, but what is the emotion? Embarrassment or anger. Why take a chance on a potentially negative approach?

Here is an example of what can happen. Take a look at Alexis. She is the new saleswoman on the team determined to make it to the top. She has set a goal for herself of selling a certain dollar amount of product on each appointment no matter what it takes. By now I hope there is a warn-ing bell going off in your head saying, "Danger, danger, **lioness** ahead." Alexis is only thinking about herself, not the customer's needs. She's ready to go out on her first appointment, or should I say hunt. She thinks she has thoroughly prepared for her meeting with Joan to present her com-plete line of We Care Cosmetics. Yes, she knows her product inside and out. As Alexis drives to Joan's house, she is dutifully reviewing all the things she's going to **tell** Joan. Alexis has set her goal, and set her mind to achieve it no matter what.

During the presentation Alexis begins to **tell** Joan, "Now dear, with your skin type it is absolutely necessary you consider nothing less than our complete skin care line."

Joan says, "Well..."

Then Alexis interrupts, "You don't want to use that same tired, dark brown colored shadow. That's what is making you look exhausted all the time. Here, use this."

Again Joan says, "Well, I really..."

Finally Aggressive Alexis interrupts one last time as she tries to make the sale, she says in frustration, "Not another word. I'm **telling** you, you'll look so good you won't recognize yourself."

About this time Joan's teenage daughter prances into the room, kisses her mother on the cheek, and expresses her excitement to look at the makeup We Care Cosmetics has to offer. The problem is Alexis has so alienated Joan that Joan is thinking of nothing other than escorting Aggressive Alexis out the door, product and all. As Alexis gets into her car, she doesn't even realize she has left something very important behind--a bad impression. Joan's daughter will buy her first complete line of cos-metics from another salesperson who really does care about her cus-tomers.

Let's examine what Alexis did wrong. First, she was not properly pre-pared for the appointment or she would have realized that it was Joan's daughter who wanted what she was offering. Joan was merely the sched-uler. The professional would have taken advantage of the possible oppor-tunity and made her offering available to both mother and daughter, let-ting each one question and convince the other. However, she would have known who the appointment was really for. She would know who was responsible for making the ultimate decision and would have at least saved face by not 'knocking' Joan's current cosmetics. Asking questions to qualify the prospect would have saved Alexis a lot of grief here. We'll talk more about qualifying questions in Chapter 4.

Next, Alexis did not practice **quiet** enthusiasm, instead she bulldozed her way in and proceeded to **tell** Joan what she needed. Alexis appealed to her customer's emotions alright--anger, hurt, and frustration. Talk about the negative sales approach.

The professional salesperson operates on a totally different concept.

If I say it, they can doubt me;

If they say it, it's true.

This is the bedrock of professional selling. It's also the foundation for the successful use of the method of guiding with questions.

Guiding Questions

Guiding with questions is a simple approach. The proper use of questions will move the selling process forward at a steady, but unpressured pace while achieving your purpose of finding out precisely what your customer needs and fears.

I strongly suggest each salesperson or company develop a list of the information required in order to make a sound recommendation of product to any client. This would be information you would need in order to call for a decision as well. Any bit of information that gets overlooked could keep the sale from going through. Also, it's vital that you take accurate notes on the information these questions provide.

Another point to cover here is that many salespeople tend to act lion-like when questioning and go for the close too soon. Be patient. This is the time to ask the who, what, where, when, and why questions that focus on customer needs instead of your need to sell. Here are just a few examples of guiding questions:

1. Who made the last purchase of a product or service of this type?
2. Who is the primary user of the product or service? How many people in the company (or the home) are affected by the purchase?

   3. What are the key concerns in making change?
   4. What do you like most about your current product and what
       would you change?
   5. What do you want to improve?
   6. What do you fear you'll lose?
   7. When do you need the product or service up and running?
   8. When can you begin training those involved?
   9. Why have you considered my particular product?
   10. How much product (quantity) do you think you will need?
   11. How do you propose to "sell" your internal staff on this change?
   12. When was the last change made and why?
   13. What colors do you like?
   14. Are there any restrictions on size?

If your prospect hesitates or seems to run out of information, use prod-
ding questions, summaries or statements that will get them to elaborate.
Some helpful phrases might sound like this:

   1. "If I understand you correctly, you are saying..."
   2. "The point then, is this..."
   3. "By this, do you mean..."
   4. "Do you think it would help if we could provide..."
   5. "Are you satisfied with your current product's ability to..."

In a sense, you need to get to your prospect's concerns about their current situation. We call the questions that bring this about <u>disturbing ques-
tions</u>. Disturbing questions are those questions that demand the buyer to
confront a problem or area of dissatisfaction about the existing product or
service, then you assume the role of problem-solver.

Another thing to be aware of when you are busy asking questions is
the non-verbal language of your customers. When you're with them
pumping out the facts, have you ever noticed how sometimes your customers will begin to pull away? If you haven't you need to brush up on
your study of body language. Don't be an aggressive, insensitive, Alexis.
Be aware of their body language. If their faces harden, their arms cross

over their chests, and you can see they have tuned you out, you need to change your approach. When this happens, you're still sending the message, but they're not receiving. You've lost them.

I think you'll agree with me that most of us are aware of body language, particularly in its most obvious forms. However, there are some more subtle forms of body language that are worthwhile for salespeople to learn. It's essential in sales that you tune in totally to the person or persons who are trying to make a buying decision. Believe me, it's worth further study if you truly have a strong desire to be successful in selling yourself, your ideas, your product or service.

When a professional talks, the sole purpose is to ask the questions and encourage the prospect to say the things that will advance the sale or let you know there is no sale. And, to ask those questions in such a manner that the prospect knows you are truly concerned for their needs. Remember, how you ask a question is as important as the question itself. Let's look at a few things the professional might say:

"You're interested in the highest quality product at a fair investment, aren't you?

Now this, of course, is a yes or no question but no one is going to answer, "No, don't give me quality. I was really looking for a piece of junk." Here's another:

"If you decided to go with this, you'd like all the protection that is included in the warranty at no additional cost, wouldn't you?"

Is anyone going to say, "Oh no. Warranties? Who needs them? If it lasts till Thursday, I'll be happy."

And again, if you word the question this way, "Working with a supplier who has a reputation for reliability and integrity is important, isn't it?" You won't find many people who would answer. "What? You have integrity and you're reliable? Get out of here!"

That's why professionals don't **tell** people, they **ask** questions. As a general rule, it's better to ask than to tell, but using questions powerfully is a bit more complicated than that.

(a) Ask the discovery questions that will reveal the benefits they'll buy so you'll know what specific products or services to provide for them, and how you can best get them involved.

(b)   Again, using the information you are gathering from your customers, ask guiding questions that will cause them to affirm their beliefs
in what they say they want, and how your product or service can provide
that for them.   They say what they want; you show them how you can
help them get it.

One more thing about asking prospects questions: Be careful when
asking questions that you don't ask anything the prospect can't answer.
How does someone feel when you ask them a question they don't know
the answer to?   How would you feel if someone came into your office for
an appointment and said, "We have three types of machines: Our G Series
with plotting and printing capability, our E Series that's plug-in programmable for over two hundred functions and operations, and our Super Z
Series that features microgrid diffraction reduction and accepts snap-on
modules for simultaneous QKD input.   Which series are you interested
in?"

Do you think the prospect will say, "Listen, I don't have a clue as to
what you just said.   Give me whatever you think is best.   Here's my
checkbook.   Fill one out and I'll sign it."   Think again.

In order to feel out whether or not you're being too technical, build
questions that give you those answers you need on your checklist we discussed earlier.   Buffer these questions with phrases such as, "Are you
familiar with......" or "Have you ever worked with......"   Simple, non-
threatening questions about their level of understanding will help you go a
long way in winning over your potential customers.

Remember, words create pictures and if a word paints no clear picture
for your client, you may lead them to confusion which will, in turn, create
a barrier between you and them.

Egos are a fragile thing.   One careless word or phrase can damage
your presentation beyond repair.   Then all you have managed to do is the
time consuming and expensive preliminary work for a truly professional
salesperson who knows the value of proper questioning techniques.   Your
slightly educated, lost customer will warm up quickly to another salesperson who knows just how to handle them at their level.   Isn't it more profitable to learn to use these methods yourself?

The professional salesperson's road is so much smoother when the customer's interest and curiosity has already been piqued by the failures of average salespeople before him. Don't spend all your time planting, only for someone else to come along and harvest your crop. Be the leader. Learn how to achieve success through the use of strong questioning methods.

When you are asked a question by a customer, take a moment to consider it before answering. Even if you have the answer at the tip of your tongue, it's often best to pause a moment to consider why they may be asking the question. What else might they have in the backs of their minds? Jumping on the question to give a quick answer doesn't always come across properly. While you may be thinking that they'll be impressed with your quick knowledge, they may be thinking you must have heard this question before or that your answer is too slick, too prepared. By pausing a moment, the prospect will get the impression that you're giving careful consideration to your answer. Depending upon the question, this could increase their perception of your level of competency as a representative of this product or service.

Always remember this: There is no such thing as a dumb question from a customer. As a matter of fact, what you think of as a really dumb question could mean an easy sale because they want it, can't think of an objection, but feel they should ask something. Let's look at the following example. The salesperson has just shown Mr. Black a home that meets all his needs and after successfully overcoming the few concerns Mr. Black has, the salesperson attempts to consummate the sale.

Salesperson: "Mr. Black, here is the list of things you said you
                    wanted in a home. I think we both agree this
                    home has everything you mentioned, doesn't it?"
Mr. Black: "Well yes, I guess so. Uh, how many times have
                    you shown this house anyway?"

The best way to address a question that seems irrelevant or unimportant is to first recognize it for what it is--a stall, a question that is asked because the customer doesn't know what else to do to allow himself a breather. The customer feels he or she should ask some questions, but doesn't really know what to ask. The salesperson could simply choose to focus on the part of Mr. Black's response that is pertinent to the sale. He has as much as said this house meets all his requirements. Such as:

Salesperson: "It's been shown to other buyers, but all home
                          buyers are different and have different needs.
                          I'm glad you agree that this home has the
                          features you are looking for. Is being in your new
                          home by Christmas still your goal?"

If Mr. Black responds with another seemingly unimportant question, then the salesperson will need to determine what is making Mr. Black uncomfortable about going ahead with his purchase of the home. What is the real objection? Obviously it is not how many times the home has been shown. So what is it?

It is often that most people don't want to be considered an easy sale. The professional recognizes their position as a facilitator, always prepared to help others succeed. The pro has learned to reserve his or her judgment, and focus on the needs and wants of the customer. The end result is quite often success.

Avoid Questions that Allow One-Word Answers

A no answer only gets you one piece of information. The more you can get your customers to say, the better your chances are to get information you can use to help them.

Try to make a game with your friends or family of questions that can't be answered by a yes or no. In fact, it often helps to turn your sales drills and practice into games. It has been said that all life is a game with rules and costs. The rules aren't always easy to follow, and the costs aren't always pleasing, but the winners accept the challenges and reap the rewards. Remind yourself that no one will be able to escape an occasional failure when they accept challenges. Here's what Walter Wriston, former chairman of Citicorp, has to say about failure. "Failure is not a crime. Failure to learn from failure is."

The Decision-Making Process

Your job as a professional salesperson is to help customers make good decisions. You are a professional problem-solver. **If you can't help them solve problems and make decisions, why do your customers need you?** They don't.

That's why I've been asking you to seek out the benefits the prospect is looking for, and then lead them to something that will provide those benefits.

Now that you have committed yourself to helping others make wise decisions, it will be beneficial for you to understand how the decision-making process works. There are, of course, variations of these steps, but when customers are faced with decisions of major consequence, they will most likely go through a similar five step process.

1. Find the facts. You want your prospects to base their decision on correct information, don't you? And, they do have a need to know what they feel is important to them about your product or service. In that case, be sure to make available to them a detailed and accurate description of your offering. If you don't know the answers to questions they ask, assure them you will find out and get back to them. This will satisfy your customer's need to find the facts.

2. Make a list. This step may not always be done in writing, but you can bet your customers will be making mental lists. They will be studying all of their options. As the customers are picturing the advantages and disadvantages of their decision, it is up to the professional salesperson to answer the objections or questions that may arise. Remember, if your prospects have no questions or objections, they are not emotionally involved with your presentation. When you have lost their attention, you may have lost the sale.

In order to address their objections, you must know what they are, you must encourage the customers to verbalize their mental lists. When they do, it's to your advantage to get permission to write that list down. It can then be used as part of the Ben Franklin decision-making tool we'll cover in Chapter 7.

3. Talk it over. If you are dealing with a group of people or a committee, this step will be obvious to you. You will often hear one prospect state his or her concerns, and if you are patient and practice calm enthusiasm and good listening habits, another prospect may answer the concern for you, thereby, reassuring one another. It is a wonderful process. This

is what often occurs in the consumer sale when it's a husband and wife doing the shopping together.

When you are working with one person, the step still occurs, however, it is mental, or done internally. Let me give you a clearer picture. Have you ever seen a cartoon where the character is trying to make a decision and he has the help of two little beings I call "Shoulder Shoulds"? One little "Shoulder Should" is portrayed as a white, soft-voiced angel telling the character how good they are, and how good people don't want to do bad things. The other little "Shoulder Should" is a little fork-tailed, red devil. This one insists that no one will ever know if the character does bad, so who cares. After all, nobody is perfect. Each is whispering into one of the cartoon character's ears. Eventually, it escalates to a shouting match.

"Yes, you should."

"Don't listen to him. Do what you want."

These same little "Shoulder Shoulds" are at work on your customers. That same type of dialog goes on inside their heads. If they are alone with their decision, they will be having this mental conversation with their invisible "Shoulder Shoulds." Wouldn't it be great if you could be the one whispering, giving advice and recommending the right decision for the customer? You can, if you get the customer to verbalize their mental conversation through the proper use of questions.

4. <u>Stand by the decision</u>. Once the customer's course of action has been decided upon, it is often difficult to change its direction in that same meeting. That is why you need to get your customers to verbalize the little arguments going on in their heads with their "Shoulder Shoulds." By getting them to talk about their doubts, you can help them overcome them. This is a good argument for not trying to close the prospect too early. The entire questioning process is a build-up to your successful close. If you cheat yourself out of yes questions, you risk cheating yourself out of a successful sale. The professional salesperson is patient and brings the prospect along at their own pace. Remember, don't **tell** the prospect what they need, let them discover it.

5. <u>Question the decision</u>. When the decision has been made, it is only natural for most prospects to question, to doubt the validity of their decision. Professionals are prepared to help the customer confront these questions and see them for what they are. Fear. The worst thing the salesperson can do at this point is cause panic. Most prospects can do a great job of that all by themselves.

Look at it this way. It is your job to patiently work with your customers helping them to take full advantage of the opportunities you have to offer. It is similar to how a parent nurtures their children. If at first a child doesn't take advantage of those things that are best for them, do you count them for lost? I'm sure you would agree with me, you wouldn't just turn around in frustration and say, "Oh well, now this one's lost. Guess I'll have to have another child to take its place so I can convince that one to experience all life has to offer."

So why do most salespeople have a similar reaction when their prospect is doubting their decision? Okay, it could be a setback, but the sale is not lost, if you learn how to handle this step with a cool head. Don't be so quick to count this prospect gone and rush out to find yourself another one. The more rebellious the child, the more reassurance is needed. The more the customer has to risk in this decision, the more reassurance they need too.

Put yourself in the place of the customer involved in the decision-making process. Let me give you another illustration. Suppose tomorrow morning you wake up with a high fever. You are miserable and you know that you are really sick. You stagger to the doctor's office and he smiles at you and says, "Hi. Thanks for coming in. You look terrible. Any idea what you have?"

"Not a clue," you say in amazement.

"Well, there's a few hundred books on the shelf behind you. Sit down, have a look and I'll be back later to see what you've found."

Even if you're sure that this time you really are dying, you are going to crawl out of there and find yourself another doctor. Why? Because you expect a professional diagnosis to satisfy your need to feel healthy again. It's the same with a prospect. They expect a professional diagnosis to provide an answer to their problem.

Champion salespeople solve product or service challenges and create opportunities for their prospects to increase productivity, enjoyment, security, income, and status, while also enjoying a host of other benefits.

The Professional Salesperson

In every case, the professional needs to have a larger base of knowledge than any one prospect can use. This means that the professional must also have a means of discovering what part of that knowledge will best serve each customer's needs. Professionals make this discovery through an organized, practiced, consultation routine. A vital element in every professional's success is the ability to define, isolate, and understand the challenges and opportunities of the customer.

Some professionals have developed a consultation routine that's deceptively casual. It appears to have no structure. Why would they do that? Because they have learned it's effective. They get more and better information from their prospects with a relaxed, offhand manner, than they do by direct questioning. Other professionals prefer, and have the skill to successfully use, a highly structured and highly visible method.

Whether the method is subtle and indirect, or brisk and to the point, professionals are always in control in a consultation interview. They know exactly what information they must learn from each customer, and they get it. They control the interview to conserve their own and their customer's time. In essence, they assist and guide the customer in the decision-making process.

Take a moment to think about how many salespeople put themselves in front of a prospect, and then let the prospect control them throughout the consultation interview. If, by chance, they do manage to move on to the presentation, it's due to the prospect's determination to buy, more than any skill the salesperson displayed. The result is that the prospect will rarely decide to obtain the benefits of their product or service because the salesperson never got the chance to properly present the benefits they would buy or ask the necessary questions. It is sad that this happens when it could be such a mutually beneficial meeting instead.

Average salespeople are quick to blame their failure on their offering. "We're just not competitive in this market." or "Our ads attract the wrong kind of leads." The problem with that argument is when you look around, if other salespeople are getting customers happily involved in that same offering and making great money at the same time, how can it be the fault of the offering? If anyone on the sales force can do it, everyone on the sales force can do it. Don't fall into the habit of blaming your product or service when you didn't get the final agreement. If you are going to make a list of all the problems that keep you from having success in selling your product or service, make sure there is a place for you on that same list.

Take every opportunity to learn more about your offering.

Better than that: *Make* opportunities to learn everything about the uses, benefits, and features of your product. Every product or service provides benefits within narrow limits, and is ineffective outside those limits. Every product or service has problems: If you attempt to ignore them, your ignorance could surface in situations that you will neither enjoy nor profit from.

Knowledge is Power

If you got into sales in order to get out of school, you'd better change your attitude. Continued education is vital to success in selling. When faced with a new educational opportunity, always remember that your competition may be there, learning what you won't.

Your first priority must be to acquire a formidable bank of expertise about what you are offering. This knowledge includes a sizable understanding of the competition and an understanding of what qualifications the prospect must have. Without such knowledge, you can't make an intelligent decision as to whether a prospect can, or should become your client.

Knowing the importance of attaining more knowledge, it is unfortunate that the majority of salespeople tend to handicap themselves intellectually by accepting the concept that once you are out of high school or college, the education process stops. It has long been believed that when you leave school, it's time to join the "real world" and go to work.

Years ago, when people saw a middle aged person furthering his or her education, what was automatically assumed? Most thought this person didn't want to face reality and get a job. We have always allowed our children the benefits of learning during their childhood, but when they became adults they somehow lost the privilege. Thank goodness this thinking is being changed by people who recognize the value of continuing education no matter what their age or position in life.

I believe learning is a necessary element in a life-long journey toward success. Whether that education is in a classroom, training seminar, or gained from listening to professionally recorded tapes or a successful co-worker, it can enhance your knowledge. Allow yourself to grow and your sales to increase by strengthening your knowledge base.

Adults learn best through practical application of their knowledge. They develop their skills by doing. Remember though, when you begin to put what you are learning to work for you, chances are you will experience some setbacks. So, accept the failures and turn them into another way to learn; turn them into opportunities. Professionals don't beat themselves down by focusing on failures. Instead, they choose to utilize the knowledge gained and move on.

Reflexive Closing Questions

Before we get into an explanation of specific selling methods, let's talk about the proper use of techniques. The ultimate goal of any professional is to become so proficient with the tools of their trade that they barely have to think about their proper use. That goes for people in the trades, doctors, dentists, artists, technicians of all types, secretaries, CPA's, cashiers -- everyone I can think of.

I want you to think about all of the sales techniques I'll teach you as tools of your trade. Your goal should be to learn to use them so well that their use becomes reflexive. In other words, you use them without having to think about their proper use. To reach this point, you must read and comprehend the material. Then, you must practice using it, preferably with friends or family members. Practice until the material feels somewhat comfortable. Once you feel comfortable with it, you will find yourself using it with customers and reaping the rewards of increased sales. The smoother the technique the more effective it will be. Now, let's get started on types of questions professionals ask.

Discovery Questions and Leading Questions

Professional salespeople use two basic types of questions:

a) **Discovery questions**

b) **Leading questions**

Some highly-skilled professionals often ask a combination of both types in one single question. The question not only leads the prospect to the decision, but it uncovers more information as well.

I find it sad, but true, that too many businesses and salespeople don't think about what they or their people are saying to customers. For example, how many times have you been browsing through a store and been asked by the salesperson, "May I help you?"

What is your standard reply? "No thanks, I'm just looking."

I don't know how many retail salespeople ask that same old tired question fifty times a day, get the same boring response fifty times a day, and they still continue asking it! As a matter of fact, many buyers have heard the question so much, they often fail to reply at all. What a ridiculous waste of time and potential.

The day salespeople stop asking the eternal say-no question, is the day they will qualify themselves to enjoy the benefits of making more sales.

Here's what I recommend salespeople say to a walk-in customer:

Salesperson: "Good morning. I work here and if you have any questions, just let me know. In the meantime, feel free to look around all you like."

Prospect: "Thank you. I was wondering, do you have..."

An example for an incoming phone contact would be:

Salesperson: "Good morning. Thank you for calling. How may I help you?"

Prospect: "Well, I was wondering, do you have..."

Sometimes the best discovery question, in the given situation, doesn't end with a question mark. It may come out as a statement, but it still gets the answer the salesperson wants. The important thing to remember is to avoid asking say-no questions. Again, the average salesperson would say: "May I quote you on your next month's requirement for envelopes?" The prospect may reply with, "No, we have all we need for some time." Instead of a say-no question, ask a discovery question.

Salesperson:	"Do you use #10 or #9 envelopes?
Prospect:	"#10."
Salesperson:	"Our rates on #10 envelopes are very competitive. Would you be offended if I send you a quote on it?"

NOTE: The way this question is worded allows them to say NO, but in this case, No gives you an affirmative to go ahead with the quote. Sometimes people feel they just have to say No. If you suspect that's the case, this is an excellent way to allow them to do so, yet still move forward in the sales process.

Notice how discovery and leading questions were used in a polite, respectful and relaxed manner. You will always remain in control of the questioning process if you calmly lead or guide your prospect with these effective techniques. Asking questions is not the only focus. Listening to their response is important too. Don't forget, it's your customer's affirmative response, or their contribution of added information that you are after.

The Porcupine Technique

If someone threw something to you and you didn't know what it was and couldn't get out of the way quickly, what would you do? If you're like most people, your reflexes would cause you to reach out to catch it and once you realized it was something you didn't want, you'd probably throw it back. All this happens in an instant. You hardly realize what you're thinking.

Of the types of questions I teach, I think this is the most potent. I call it the porcupine because I want you to envision a little porcupine shuffling around in the brush with its sharp quills sticking out. If someone picked it up and threw it at you, what would you do? You'd throw it right back, wouldn't you?

The porcupine technique is that of answering a prospect's question with a question of your own. You do this in such a polite and courteous manner that the prospect ignores the fact that you didn't directly answer their question. For example, "When can we get it?" is a common question that is perfect for throwing the porcupine back to the buyer:

Prospect: "Could we have it delivered by the first of the month?"

You: (Smile) "Does delivery by the first of the month best suit your needs?"

Using the porcupine technique keeps you in command of the interview and allows you to guide your prospects to the next step of your selling sequence.

You may ask, "Won't the prospect be annoyed unless I give them specific answers to their questions?"

If it's done smoothly and reflexively, they probably won't. You'll simply be asking a question to clarify further what it is they're asking. It can become annoying if you overuse the porcupine questioning method or any of the methods we'll cover in the rest of this book. As you become more professional, you will carry with you all the skills necessary to make the sale, and be flexible to use any skill or combination of skills as needed. The key is becoming adept at delivering them with so much politeness, warmth and courtesy that the fact you're using a sales system never dawns on them. To the prospect, you will simply sound self-assured and confident. When you easily and calmly respond to their question with another question, the prospect won't be thinking, "Oh, this clever salesperson has learned the porcupine question method." They will be too busy thinking of their next response.

Practice using the porcupine with your family or friends. They will help you use this skill in an effective manner, without fear of annoying your prospect.

In any type of sales work, you'll constantly encounter questions that you can answer yes or no to, and end up with nothing. You'll also be asked to give all the information that you can give, and this too will cause you to end up with nothing. The porcupine question method is a helpful tool to use while building your overall sales skills.

Learning some of these methods is much like learning to drive using a manual shift car on the expressway during rush hour. Don't put yourself in this position. Practice on the back streets first, with people who will let you make mistakes. Then go out and merge into traffic at a pace that is comfortable for you.

Back to the professionals. Professional salespeople use the porcupine because it helps them determine what the prospect is looking for.

Let's look at two more porcupines:

Prospect:	"Does this product have one of those extended warranties?"
Salesperson:	"Is having an extended warranty important to you?"
Prospect:	"Definitely not. I think they're useless."
Salesperson:	"May I ask why you feel that way?"

We all have preconceived notions about things. Your prospect may have a preconceived notion about warranties. They may have had a bad past experience with a warranty or they may not even truly understand what the extended warranties can do for them. Isn't it vital to find out things like that? With this prospect, if you try to sell the extended warranty, you may sell yourself straight into a brick wall.

But if he said, "I want all the warranty I can get." Then you know how to shape the rest of your presentation, don't you?

If your prospect says, "Can we get this one in pink?" What porcupine would you use?

If you have it in pink, you could say, "Does the color pink best suit the room you'll be using it in?" Of course, if the product only comes in red, white and blue, you would need to ask another question, "Is color your primary concern in the purchase of this item?" Their answer will tell you how far you will have to go to get the final agreement, or if they would never consider the product in red, white or blue. Using porcupines will get you the information. Porcupines are also used as test closes. These are questions you would ask to test the waters -- to see how close your prospect is to making a buying decision.

The Champion salesperson understands how warmly the porcupine can be used, and how important it is to ask porcupine questions with an air of warm and friendly interest. Remember, the value of the porcupine is destroyed if overused. Always deliver it in a warm, friendly tone and not with a challenging "put-up or shut-up" attitude. **Quiet power** is the name of the game.

The Alternate Advance Question

The alternate advance is a question that suggests two answers, both of which confirm that your prospect is going ahead. These are questions that cannot be answered yes or no to, but give the prospect a choice: Either choice will bring an answer that tells you the prospect is willing to keep moving ahead. You can use the alternate advance in minor situations, and in the final closing sequence.

In most kinds of sales work, it's almost impossible to finalize the sale without first getting an appointment with the buyer. Because of this, it's vital that you don't lose appointments unnecessarily, and get stopped before you can start. This is why a Champion would never say, "Can I come by this afternoon?"

If you were a busy executive, what would you say? "No, I've got a heavy schedule today. I'll call you when I have more time." Don't hold your breath.

A professional salesperson gives the prospect two options:

"Mr. Johnson, I'll be in your area this afternoon. Which time would be more convenient for me to stop by 2:00, or would you prefer 3:30?" The customer will either make a choice or give you an objection. This type of question shows that you are willing to serve them at their convenience -- that you are being flexible for them.

When he or she answers, "Three-thirty would be better," you have an appointment. You got it by suggesting two yeses instead of a no. As you go through these, I'm sure you will agree, these alternate advances are great. Take a look at the next one:

"Mr. and Mrs. Summers, let's set up your delivery date. Which is best for you, the first or the tenth?"

"Oh, we need it by the first." When they've told you that, you know they are at least on their way to owning it in their minds, but the sale may not be complete at this point. If your product or service requires some kind of deposit, put your request for it in the form of an alternate advance.

Let's look at a $3 million jet for example. Before you let your prospect fly the aircraft, you've qualified them, haven't you?

If you said: "What type of deposit would you like to put down?" Some people might pull out a $50 bill and say, "Here. I'll take the jet." So, instead you say, "As you know, we have a substantial investment here. Which would you prefer, a 20 or 30 percent deposit?" Which one will they choose? It doesn't matter, as long as they choose one.

So, the alternate advance is any question that gives your prospect two alternatives and either of those alternatives confirms that they are going ahead, or if they are indifferent to both alternatives you may have an objection to address but either way, you are still moving forward in the selling process.

The Involvement Question

You may already be using this question without realizing that this is an important technique with a long history of success. If the involvement question came to you naturally, great. Let your previous success with it encourage you to work this method harder.

Weave involvement questions into all your presentations and you'll find yourself making more sales.

An involvement question is any positive question about the bene-fits of your product or service that buyers must ask themselves after they own it.

In other words, an involvement question is an ownership question. Remember those key words. You want your prospects to **own** your product or service, not to **buy** it. Think about the pictures those two words conjure up. "Buy" brings to mind pictures of money being spent, cash leaving your pocket or purse. "Own" brings to mind pictures of pride, enjoyment, satisfaction, benefits. We'll discuss this idea of using word pictures more in Chapter 6.

When you ask an involvement question before they own your product or service, their answer confirms whether or not they are going ahead. Let's try this on the owner of the business who is considering that $3 million jet.

"Mr. Myers, will you be using the plane for company business only, or would you consider leasing it out?"

That's an alternate advance question, isn't it? But it's also an involvement question. Notice how the professional has worded the involvement question so as to point out a benefit of owning the offering. Mr. Myers can reduce the cost of ownership considerably by chartering the jet when his business isn't using it, and you want him to know about this option before he makes the decision to invest in it. This causes him to think ownership thoughts--thoughts of what he will do *after* he owns the jet.

Involvement questions can be created for every product or service. You have a challenge, and an obligation, to develop involvement questions for your offering--a challenge because not every product lends itself to this technique with equal ease, an obligation because you can't operate at your most effective level unless you create involvement questions to help your prospects own your product or service. Your opportunity with the involvement question, and all the other skills in this book, is to create something that leads you to fulfilling your customers' needs, getting more people happily involved in your product or service, thus increasing your own personal wealth. The more service you provide, the greater chance you have to create personal wealth.

Tiny Questions that Build Momentum

The Standard Tie-Down
    A tie-down is a question at the end of a sentence that demands a "Yes" answer. Here's an example:
    "Cost control is very important today, isn't it?"
    If what you said represents truth as the prospect sees it, won't that person respond by agreeing? When the prospect agrees that some quality of your product or service fits their needs, they've moved closer to a positive final agreement, haven't they? Use of the tie-down enables you to get agreement or pop an objection. If they disagree with your tie-down, you'll know to alter your course covering that point in more depth or avoiding it entirely.
    Here are eighteen standard tie-downs that you will find valuable:

Wouldn't it?	Couldn't it?	Shouldn't it?
Wasn't it?	Won't they?	Won't you?
Isn't it?	Didn't it?	Doesn't it?
Haven't they?	Hasn't he?	Hasn't she?
Aren't they?	Aren't you?	Can't you?
Isn't that right?	Don't we?	Don't you agree?

There are others, of course, but these will give you a good start--or should I say a good end. Place these on the end of your sentences and you'll gather lots of minor yeses. Selling is the art of asking the right questions to get the minor yeses that allow you to lead your prospect to the major decision and the major yes.

Here are some other tie-down sentences. Practice the technique by filling in the blanks as you read the following sentences:

Example: "Cost control is very important today, **isn't it**?"

1. "Most companies are investing heavily in high-tech equipment today, _____?"
2. "It would be very convenient to have your own cellular phone, _____?"
3. "Taking care of your family is very important, _____?"
4. "They're fun, _____?"
5. "It just takes practice, _____?"
6. "They're becoming natural now, _____?"
7. "You'd like to enjoy the best that life has to offer, _____?"
8. "A professional can do several things at once, _____?"
9. "With a bit of practice, tie-downs will come to you easily, _____?"
10. "Tie-Downs are questions that will lead your clients toward the decision to enjoy the benefits of your product or service, _____?"
11. "You are a Champion, _____?"
12. "These are easy, _____?"

Those sentences demonstrate the use of the standard tie-down. I'm certain with a little thought you will come up with many more for your own product or service.

The Inverted Tie-Down

For variety and more warmth, you can put the tie-down at the beginning of the sentence. Before you decide that this is too simple to practice, consider that we're talking about a tool you will use in a fast and demanding sales situation. A good mixture of the four tie-down types won't find their way into your sales situations by accident. A Champion can smoothly weave all four tie-down types in and out of the conversation without hesitation. To do this requires a skill level that demands rehearsal.

Use the tie-down exercise sentences for inverted form practice.

Standard tie-down: "Quality is what you're looking for, isn't it?"

Inverted tie-down: "Isn't quality what you're looking for?"

The prospect may say, "Yes, quality is what I'm looking for, but price is the most important thing for me." So now you've gotten even more information.

The Internal Tie-Down

The internal tie-down is placed in the middle of the sentence. This is easier than it sounds. Here's a look at the standard, the inverted, and the internal:

Standard:

"Tie-downs are easy once you get a feel for them, aren't they?"

Inverted:

"Aren't they easy, once you get a feel for them?"

Internal:

"Tie-downs are easy, aren't they, once you get a feel for them?"

Another variation of the internal form is:

"Once you get a feel for them, aren't tie-downs easy?

To change any simple tie-down sentence into the internal form, hang a phrase on the beginning or end of it. Take the shortest of the tie-down exercise sentences, "They're fun, aren't they?" Hook a phrase on the front and you've got a complex sentence and an internal tie-down: "Once you get used to them, aren't they fun?"

The Tag-On Tie-Down

Our last tie-down question is a great agreement momentum-builder. It's used in a variety of ways. In its simplest form, you tag your tie-down onto any statement your prospect happens to make that is positive.

Prospect: "Time saving is so important."

You: "Isn't it?"

The customer said it, so to the customer, it's true. Without sounding repetitive, tie down things the prospect says that may be helpful to the sale. You will then get a positive minor agreement, won't you?

You caught the tie-down in the last sentence, didn't you? That's great, isn't it? That means your reflexes are tuned in for the use of tie-downs.

Don't you agree that sales opportunities can be gained or lost in a moment? They can, can't they?

Here's an example of tag-along questions working off tag-on tie-downs. The prospect has come into your showroom and the matter of color comes up:

Prospect: "I like red."
You: "Isn't red a wonderful color? We're offering a choice of
                three new shades of red this year. Would you prefer Really
                Red, Burning Red, or Red, Red Wine?"
Prospect: "I think I like Burning Red. It's beautiful."
You: "Isn't it?"

When you've trained yourself to recognize opportunities for tag-along questions, you can warmly use the proper tie-down and think about a tag-along question that will both hold the prospect's interest and lead them closer to the big decision.

Opportunities for tag-on-tie-downs come and go quickly, so training yourself to snap them up is important. It is important to realize that even though there seem to be some people who get all the breaks, there are more of us who make our own breaks. As you train your ear to recognize these tie-downs, you train your mind and mouth to practice them. Fortunately, that's easy. Use your radio. Normally, I recommend against listening to the radio while driving to work or to appointments. That's the time you should be listening to sales or motivational tapes. However, in this case, you can use your local talk radio station to practice your skills with tie-down.

Practice all the tie-down variations. Experiment with them on your friends, family members or anyone you meet with throughout the day until they become a habit. I found it great fun to use them to get my children to do things when they were young. "Having a clean room is much more fun than not being able to find things in a messy room, isn't it?" They're also helpful in getting a group of friends to agree on where to go out. "We had great fun going to dinner there the last time, didn't we?"

Create, practice, drill, and rehearse fifteen tie-down questions of your own. Then do fifteen more. Remember to mix all four types throughout the conversation. Also, be careful not to overuse the tie-down. Don't get carried away. Overuse may hurt you. Any speech pattern when overused, can become annoying. I'm sure you know people who continually inter-ject sounds, words or phrases such as: you know, like, literally, and uh into every conversation.

Overuse of questioning methods will trigger customer suspicions that you may be using a canned technique -- that you may not be sincere. If the person listening to you hears the same word or phrase overly used, they begin to wonder why you keep saying those things. This often trig-gers a certain degree of fear that you are using a rehearsed presentation or using technique on them.

The true key to success in applying any of the methods given in this book is in the style of delivery and blending of techniques. That's also why I stress that you must internalize the material. Make it a natural part of you. If you are sincere in your concerns for giving your customers the best product or service, this will come easily to you.

When you have practiced to the point where you feel relaxed and comfortable, plan a practice presentation with a friend or family member. Act exactly as if you were speaking with a prospect. Try different situa-tions. For example, make one situation an attempt to get an appointment. Another practice could include a presentation to persuade your prospect to own your product or service and eventually approve your agreement. Remember, a sale depends on getting agreement and all you are trying to do with these little points is to get small agreements that will build into a bigger agreement -- the agreement to own your product or service.

It would be a good idea to tape these different situations. When you are nervous or excited, you can't get a true perspective on your approach. Believe me, the tape will point out the good, bad, and the ugly. Don't be discouraged if you have difficulty the first time around. Keep an open ear for the perfect message. Grade your performance realistically. If you persevere, all your hard work will pay off. Those wonderful rewards you thought were reserved for the select few Champions can be yours.

The Importance of Note Taking

After investing all that time learning the proper questions to ask, you don't want to miss the major point of it all, do you? Asking the right questions is essential for one and only one reason -- to hear the answers. When you hear those answers, do whatever you must to get them written down as soon as possible.

Don't depend on your memory. I'm sure, if you are like me, your memory has been inaccurate at times. If you fail to take notes on the little things, how can you expect to serve all your customer's needs?

Your memory can give you a picture of past events, but the scene is rarely picture perfect. It's often somewhat distorted. You'll often fill in details the way you would have liked them to be, instead of how things really were. There can be a big disparity between what you **remember** happening and what actually happened.

What would happen if you depended on your memory, and the details of a particular meeting were a bit fuzzy? It would be awkward to say the least, and extremely unprofessional.

Professional salespeople are always challenged to find ways to consummate the agreement. Sometimes looking back at your notes might lead you in a direction you had not previously thought of. Besides, you may be working with many prospects, each one having a variety of needs. How will you make sure to keep all the information straight if you don't devise an organized note-taking routine? A few moments of note-taking can often save you the embarrassment of not being able to recall those details that tell your prospect your meeting with them was a memorable experience. The whole sales process is a successful cycle of gathering information that leads to the fulfillment of your customer's needs. Don't wing it! Write it!

CHAPTER 3
ORIGINAL CONTACT, BUILDING RAPPORT

At your first contact with a prospective new client, what are your predominant thoughts? Are you thinking about closing the sale? Are you thinking about how you look? Or, are you thinking that this could be the start of a beautiful relationship? Hopefully, you will always remind yourself to think of the latter just before meeting a prospect.

Building rapport, the getting-to-know-you phase of selling, is highly critical. What happens in the first few moments of this stage will establish the foundation for any future relationship. We all know that we never get a second chance to make a positive first impression. So, why don't we prepare more for that first impression? Anyone involved in sales needs to learn more and better ways to make this stage of the sale the smoothest, most comfortable situation you and your prospect have ever been involved in.

Rapport building can be compared to laying the foundation of a new building. You are laying the foundation for new sales -- not only from this client, but from potentially hundreds of people they could refer to you over the years.

What is the definition of rapport? Webster says it is: **Harmonious mutual understanding; the state of individuals who are in utter agreement.** Isn't that a wonderful position to be in with your customers--"harmonious mutual understanding." So, now that we understand what rapport is, how do we establish it? Let me give you three easy steps to help you establish good rapport:

1. <u>Use their name as they give it</u>. Many people want to shorten first names in hopes of establishing that friendly rapport with their customers. Be careful. This could be a dangerous practice. I have to admit I was guilty of this in my early years of selling. I would often shorten Michael to Mike, or Richard to Dick. There is a reason why people tell you their names in full, usually it is because that is how they expect you to use them. Maybe later in the relationship when you have earned the privilege of being a bit more familiar, you can use the familiar form, but only after you have earned it. Most customers will let you know if and when that's a possibility. You walk a fine line in rapport-building. Remember, you are not trying to become the prospect's new best friend. You are trying to establish a professional relationship in which they see you as an expert whose advice they can benefit from. You need to keep your relationship-building on that professional level. You want to come across as not just a warm, wonderful, person, but a highly skilled professional who can help them -- someone they can trust.

2. <u>Ask for permission to use their first name, if they give you both the first and last names</u>. I know this sounds like an old-fashioned practice, but sometimes those traditional values show respect and consideration; two of today's most underrated traits. A good practice to adopt is to use their last names a few times at the beginning of your presentation, then ask them if they would be offended if you called them by their first names. If you have earned their trust and respect, if you have established good rapport, the permission you seek should be forthcoming.

3. <u>Establish common ground or mutual acquaintances</u>. This is a wonderful tool you can use to help build good rapport, but be careful. The danger is that you often spend too much time in this process, at the expense of time needed for your presentation. It takes just a few moments to find common ground, don't allow yourself to lose sight of the reason you are there. Probably the easiest, and most over-looked way to establish common ground is to take a good look at your prospect's office.

What's on the walls? What type of magazines are in the lobby? This is often an indication of where their interests lie. Do they have pictures on their desk? If the pictures are of family members, comment on what a good looking family they have. It's really easy if you are just observant.

Another good way to find out what you might have in common is to simply ask questions. For example, you might ask where they are from, then relate a little story about when you traveled in that part of the country. Remember, when you draw pictures with your words, make them positive pictures.

If you've never been there ask them what it's like or what they liked about living there. Be careful not to ask why they moved.

It could have been a forced move by the company or the result of a personal relationship upheaval. You don't want to dredge up any negative feelings here.

Take a look at this rapport-setting introduction:

"You know Mr. Johnson, when I'm not helping people get involved with my product, I'm a consumer just like you, looking for quality products at the best price. What I hope for when I'm shopping is to find someone who can help me understand all the facts about the item I'm interested in so I can make a wise decision.

Today, I'd like to earn your trust in me as an expert on (Put your product or service in this space. Make the words yours). So feel free to ask any questions you might have."

Notice how I used the term "price" instead of "investment." "Price" is not a term professionals use in referring to the money part of a transaction. We'll cover this more in-depth in Chapter 6. It's OK to use "price" here because you have not yet educated your customer about what a wise "investment" it will be to "own" your product. Take a moment now and write an introduction for yourself that will show warmth, and concern; or that will be a good rapport builder.

Actions that Help Establish Rapport

1. <u>Don't walk directly toward the customer as they enter your establishment</u>.

If you are involved in sales that require you to approach your customers on a show room floor, or in a large open space, we recommend you avoid the direct path. If this is not contrary to company policy, walk around to the side so they will not feel like you are in hot pursuit or that you'll block any attempt they may make to walk through the store unattended. When you approach them head-on, it's like a red-flag signal saying, "You're mine" and they'll certainly get an image of dollar signs in your eyes.

2. <u>Sit or stand beside them</u>. If you are looking at a product or literature for your service, standing or sitting beside them says,"We're on the same team. We're looking at this from the same point of view."

3. <u>Work on developing a flexible personality</u>. Over the years, we have identified nine personality types of buyers ;with which you should familiarize yourself. Listed below are these personality types and some suggestions of what to do when you encounter them.

Personality Types of Buyers
   A) <u>Believing Bart</u>
He is already sold on your company. He is easy to manage and loyal once you have convinced him of your personal worth. If he is not convinced of your worth, he will be the first one to call your company and request another representative. How do you appeal to this type? You will need to exhibit great product knowledge to build trust and belief in your ability to meet his needs. Another important element in consummating this sale and gaining repeat business will be to provide dependable service and follow-up.
   B) <u>Freddie Freebie</u>
He is a real "wheeler-dealer" who won't settle until he thinks he
has the upper hand and you've agreed to give him something extra. Today's market is full of these types. If you give him any extras in order to consummate the sale, it's highly likely he will brag to and upset others who may not have received the same benefit. How do you handle this type? Make him feel he is important and special -- that he drives a hard bargain and that you admire his business savvy. If you feel his business is worth giving something extra, consult with your manager or the business owner.

C) Purchasing Polly

She is a rather distant, matter-of-fact type who carries a high level of responsibility. Polly, as well as many other purchasing agents, may have little personal contact throughout the day other than with the endless stream of salespeople who parade through her office. She can't risk liking you too much because she could have to replace you with the competition at any time. How do you handle this type? This should be a no-fluff presentation. Don't try to become too familiar. Stick to the facts and figures. By being low-key, you'll be different from all the other 'typical' salespeople she encounters. She'll remember you for that. Let her know you understand how important and challenging her position may be. Send thank you notes. Present all figures in the most professional manner possible. Do everything in writing.

D) Evasive Ed

He is one of the most challenging. He refuses to return your phone calls. He postpones appointments or reschedules at the last minute. He likes to shop around, and keeps you waiting in the meantime. How do you handle this type? Enlist the aid of his secretary or support staff. They may be able to tell you how to get and keep his business.

E) Griping Greg

He always has something to complain about. Very negative person. You have to question whether he is worth all the energy he will steal from you. How do you handle his type? The most important thing you can do is listen and be empathetic. To keep your accessibility to his negativity brief, I recommend that you only call him a few minutes before his normal lunch hour or just before the end of the day, so he won't want to talk long. If he calls you at other times and begins to cost you valuable selling time, you'll have to learn polite ways to get off the line. When you first get on the line, say something like this: "Greg, I'm so glad you called. I'm just heading out for an appointment, what can I do for you in the next five minutes?" Try to remain pleasant and helpful, after all that's why Ed still gives you his business. If Ed gets to be too much to handle, the easiest and least costly thing to do might be to refer him to someone else in your organization.

F) <u>Anna List</u>

She knows exactly what she wants. She will knit-pick everything.
She is extremely insecure. Usually she is very afraid of losing her job, so
she is big on complete control. How do you handle this type? First of all
be very organized. She will appreciate this quality. Handle every detail
in writing. Another important point is to be punctual. Double check
everything. Confirm appointments, re-confirm details of your meetings
with her in writing. I recommend sending a recap of every meeting via
facsimile. Fax ahead to let her know what information you'll be bringing
to your next appointment. In other words, treat her as she is. Everyone
wants to be around people 'just like them.'

G) <u>Domineering Donna</u>

She is a strong willed ball-of-fire. She will often not reveal her needs
because she will expect that if you have done your homework, you'll
already know them. How do you handle this type? One of the most
important things to do is compliment her on her importance -- the value of
her abilities to her company. Remember, it's likely she treats everyone
like this and most people will avoid working with dominators. You can't.

Besides, she can become a positive force for you if you have challenges with billing or want to sell your product to another   department or
branch of the company.

H) <u>Controlling Carl</u>

It's his way or the highway. He's a self-proclaimed expert. He's also
poor at delegating authority. He wants everyone and everything being
reported to him. He may be rude and interrupt your presentation while he
takes calls or gives directions to his secretary. How do you handle him?
You must be extremely polite. Be very prepared and concise. Don't
assume anything. Let him know you value his time. If the interruptions
become too distracting, offer to re-schedule your meeting off premises so
you can have his undivided attention. Or, enlist the aid of his secretary or
assistant in keeping interruptions to a minimum.

I) <u>Cynical Cindy</u>

She is first to say, "Well, we've always done it this way." She fights
change. She is suspicious and questions your every move. How do you
handle this type? Welcome her objections, even brag that she was smart

enough to bring that up. Use the Higher Authority closing technique on Cindy that we'll cover in Chapter 7. The great thing about Cindy is if you have such a difficult time overcoming her objections you can be assured your competition may get discouraged trying to win her over. She will be a hard one for your competition to persuade to change her loyalties.

Most of us have an innate instinct about others, but we aren't always conscious of it. It's important to pay attention to this instinct, especially if you want to succeed in sales. As with anything, I don't recommend over-doing it on body language or instinct, but it's wise to study it and develop it to the level it serves you best.

Highlight this and remember it when you are having an especially difficult time with one of these personality types. The more difficult the personality, the better client they are likely to become once you win them over. I hope you realize the necessity of having a flexible personality that enables you to relate to all different personality types. Remember, if you can't like the personality, learn to like the opportunity they are offering you to practice the skills that will make you a Champion.

4. <u>Develop sensitivity to your customers</u>. Do your customers feel important around you? If not, you haven't been doing your job. Champions have empathy for their customers and they do not hesitate to show it. Think of yourself as a teacher. It is your job to care for their personal growth while educating them about your product or service. One of the best ways to build rapport is to ask questions about their specific needs, listen to the answers and take notes to demonstrate your desire for accuracy in every aspect of business. Everyone loves having someone sincerely interested in their needs and desires. The primary element of empathetic behavior is to be a good listener. Below are the three types of listeners:

A) <u>Empathetic</u>

This professional pays total attention to what is being said. They are able to block out all distractions. They watch body language carefully and catch the meaning conveyed in the speaker's tone of voice.

B) <u>Average</u>

These salespeople hear the words but they are not getting the whole picture. They fail to read between the lines to discover what their customers really want and need.

C) <u>Poor</u>

These salespeople experience difficulty, often drifting into day- dreaming. They only half listen, so when they need to recall important facts, they come up short.

Since developing good listening skills is extremely important to professional salespeople, let me show you some of the reasons many salespeople have difficulty in this area.

1. <u>Fatigue</u>

Salespeople often experience fatigue because they are asked to give so much of themselves in the process of selling. Many times you find yourself working long hours, and during your off time, you need to continually research and study to improve your techniques. Know your energy level. Nobody functions best when they are tired. Most everyone has a time of day when they are more alert. Be aware of when this time is for you, and learn to schedule your most critical presentations during your most productive time.

Another thief of energy is bad news. Do you realize how you are bombarded by bad news every day? Bad news fills the newspapers, TV news broadcasts, radio programming--it's everywhere. Avoid it as much as possible. Listen to motivational tapes in your car. Balance your TV and radio programming with uplifting books and quality music. At least you will be doing something to replenish the energy bad news steals from you.

A third cause of fatigue is people. We all know certain people who drain our energy. This includes people who thrive on gossip. These people should be avoided any time it could affect your ability to sell.

Fatigue is also a sign of being out of balance. If there are areas of your life in which you are less than fulfilled, that void will begin to drain on you. Take a few moments every week to feel yourself out and make plans for activities in any of the areas in which you feel you are lacking. In other words, do something about it!

2. External Distractions

One of the worst things that can happen during a presentation is to be constantly interrupted. Not only does this break the entire rhythm of your presentation, but it's annoying and negative emotions block your ability to concentrate on your listening. If you foresee a situation where you will have these distractions, it is best to reschedule the appointment at a different time and location where these distractions will not have a chance to inflict damage.

For example, I know of a top saleswoman who would always arrange her meetings at a local restaurant, where both she and her clients were not distracted with phone calls or demanding children. She had a master plan. She notified the restaurant ahead of time, letting them know that she would be coming for a quiet business luncheon at a scheduled time that afternoon. She always patronized the same restaurant, knowing that her privacy and quiet time would be respected by the owners and help. Lastly, she was always careful to tip well, insuring a continued working relationship with this establishment.

3. Time Lag

This term refers to how fast one can speak compared with how fast one can comprehend. The average person can hear and comprehend between 300-500 words per minute. The average person speaks at a rate of approximately 150-200 words per minute. What do you do with the difference that's called time lag? If you give the customers too much time to allow their minds to wander, they will do just that. They will begin to think about their next appointment or meeting, the work they should be getting finished, what they will eat for dinner, or even worse, how they will get out of this situation. That is why you must know your product and techniques so well, that your words easily flow one to another without uncomfortable hesitation or pause.

4. Meaning Of Words

This is one of the easiest ways to keep your customers from listening to you--use words they don't understand. Not only will they stop listening to you, but they will become aggravated or annoyed with the whole presentation. This is the whole point of communication. Words should be used to create pictures. If you use words that do not create images that are common to most people, they will be lost, trying to find an image to fit their understanding of what you said and miss the next few points. The same thing happens when your customer uses trade talk that you aren't familiar with. Take a close look at your presentation, even tape record it if possible. Have someone who is unfamiliar with your product, service or industry listen to it and identify any words they need defined. Then, in future presentations, give the definition of those terms the first time you use them. This is a tremendous communication-building tactic.

5. Not Watching Body Language

Get accustomed to observing your customer's body language. Did you know that half of our messages are non-verbal? The following are some clues about how to read body language and what to do when you see them.

Body Language Cues
A) Hands are open and relaxed. Palms are turned upward and the per son shrugs.
   What's happening? They are open, relaxed.
   What to do? Mirror them. Don't shrug, but sit back with your hands open and relaxed.
B) Does not make eye contact.
   What's happening? They don't like you or something you've just said.
   What to do? Smile. Try to win their trust. If necessary review the last point. Ask if something about that point is bothering them. Talk about your desire to make them happy.
C) Jacket unbuttoned and later removed.
   What's happening? They are getting down to business, but they are comfortable.
   What to do? Mimic their actions as far as you are comfortable. Be certain to get their permission to remove your jacket or other wise get more comfortable.

D) The customer moves closer.
   <u>What's happening</u>? They trust you.
   <u>What to do</u>? Attempt to close if the timing is right.
E) Faces and looks intently at speaker. Head is slightly tilted.
   Touches chin or side of face.
   <u>What's happening</u>? Very interested.
   <u>What to do</u>? Continue with presentation and prepare for a trial close.
F) Removes eyeglasses, wipes off lenses. May put ear piece in mouth.
   <u>What's happening</u>? Pausing for thought. Wants to slow things down.
   <u>What to do</u>? Slow the pace down. Clarify your previous point. Summarize and repeat benefits already agreed to. Ask if there are any questions.
G) Raised eyebrows, wrinkles forehead, jaw drops open.
   <u>What's happening</u>? Surprised, startled.
   <u>What to do</u>? First, determine if the reaction is positive or negative. If it is negative, calm them down. If it is positive, excite them further.
H) Pulls on ear while another talks.
   <u>What's happening</u>? Wants to break into the conversation.
   <u>What to do</u>? Pause, then ask if they have a question.
I) Leaning back in chair. Hands with fingertips together.
   <u>What's happening</u>? High degree of self-confidence.
   <u>What to do</u>? Acknowledge their superiority. Let their ego puff up. Compliment them. Reinforce their good feelings.
J) Hand covers mouth while speaking.
   <u>What's happening</u>? Uncertain. Self-doubt.
   <u>What to do</u>? Reassure and clarify points. Recap or cover it in another way. Ask if they have any questions or concerns.
K) Squirming around in chair.
   <u>What's happening</u>? Feeling pressure. Uncomfortable.
   <u>What to do</u>? Use humor if possible. Lighten up. Suggest taking a break, if possible.

L) Repeatedly clicking ball point pen. Tapping feet on floor, drawing designs on table with finger.

<u>What's happening</u>? Impatient or bored.

<u>What to do</u>? Change subject. Take a break if necessary. Change pace.

M) Playing with paper clip or other small article. Eyes lowered during discussion.

<u>What's happening</u>? Insecure, unsure, prejudging.

<u>What to do</u>? Reassure them. Offer to explain in greater detail. Give recognition. Make them feel important.

Although these are not 100% accurate, as a general rule you can depend on them to alert you to potential problems.

Each of the areas discussed in this chapter could be expanded into a book of its own. Rather than go into great detail, we chose to give you highlights of each area. If you desire to study any of the areas in further detail, you will likely find volumes of material on body language in your local bookstore or library. Again, don't get hung up on this topic. After all it is an innate ability. Simply gaining a better awareness of it will be a tremendous benefit to your entire career.

CHAPTER 4
QUALIFICATION

Evaluations of selling skills of over 350,000 salespeople have shown us that the most critical lack of skill is in the area of qualification. The ability to qualify prospective buyers can save you hours of valuable selling time and help you earn much higher income. If you are not a good qualifier, you will need to be an excellent objection-handler because there are certain aspects of every buyer's needs that must be addressed sooner or later. I teach my students effective qualifying methods so they can get to those points sooner and to save them the time they could have wasted preparing for and demonstrating to unqualified buyers.

Have You Ever...

Let's take a few minutes and play "Have you ever..." I'm sure as you read through many of these questions asking if you have ever had similar experiences, you will be nodding your head in agreement. If you can answer yes to any of the following questions, you have just added your support to the importance of and need to qualify. Let me ask you the following:

* <u>Have you ever</u> spent hours explaining your product or service only to discover the person you were presenting your offering to was not the decision-maker?
* <u>Have you ever</u> carefully prepared one copy of your complete presentation, only to find out your meeting is with a large group or committee?

*   <u>Have you ever</u> enthusiastically presented your top-of-the-line offering
    with all the bells and whistles, only to be told by the customer that
    what they were really looking for was the basic model?
*   <u>Have you ever</u> recommended what you know would be a dynamite
    product or service for your prospect, only to hear the discouraging
    words, "Oh, we tried that before and it was a disaster"?

These time wasting irritants for both you and the customer tell the
story of why you must practice proper qualification. Qualifying a customer is not done to simply make friendly conversation with the customer,
or to break the ice. That's not to say the customer won't feel like you are
making friendly conversation when you ask your qualifying questions in a
lamb-like manner, but there must be a definite purpose or plan behind the
questions you ask. That purpose is to discover the customer's needs. If
your questions have no focus, your customer will also have trouble focusing on the business at hand. They may even wonder why all the questions, or just what it is that you are getting at. But, before you delve into
learning the proper way to qualify potential customers, you must first
qualify yourself as a salesperson.

Qualify Yourself as a Salesperson
    Qualifying is a process of looking for answers. For example, just to
help you understand, let's ask you some questions about qualifying yourself as a salesperson. In order to qualify yourself, you must know your
own career expectations, personal needs, and emotional wants. Let's
begin with the questions to ask yourself in order to do just that.

Personal Qualification Questions
    Begin each question with, "WHAT AM I...

    1. <u>Willing to do</u>? Are you willing to do the things that you know you
should do to be successful? This is perhaps one of the most important
questions of your sales career. So the simple question is, are you? Are
you willing to study, drill, and practice? Are you willing to make all the
sacrifices that will be required of you to be successful in sales? Are you

willing to put yourself in potentially uncomfortable situations? If you say
yes to a long term commitment in selling, you must set up and follow the
short term steps necessary to help you do what you know you should,
including training.

2. Assured of? This is difficult to answer. Can anyone guarantee
another's success? No, but we can do the next best thing. We can teach
you to guarantee your own success. If you do what we teach and you
know you should, you can increase your success ratio. Sure, you probably won't be successful every time, but your percentage of success will
increase dramatically. When this happens, you will find the added motivation to examine what needs improving, and do what you know you
should--improve your selling skills. You then build a successful sales
cycle.

3. Not able to achieve, and why do I believe this? Often times when
we believe something to be true, it is. You have certain perceptions of
yourself. These self-perceptions have been developed and fed throughout
your lifetime by you and all those surrounding you. If you truly believe
there are things impossible for you to achieve, give up the dream. Don't
waste your time pursuing something you don't believe in. Another little
piece of advice: Surround yourself with people who believe in you. That
kind of energy is very contagious. Soon you will be on the bandwagon of
your own personal support group.

4. Telling myself every day? This is somewhat linked to number
three. Simply put, are you reinforcing the negative or the positive? Make
it the positive, and I'm sure your sales results will change for the better.
Remember, if you say it, you own it.

5. Selling? This is one of the most important concepts to grasp.
While it is obvious you are selling your product or service, it is most
important to sell your prospect on you and your company as well.
Remember what we said about letting your customer be the star?
Consider their benefit in every word you speak. Put your own needs

behind that of your customers, and you will be selling yourself as someone who is truly concerned about what's in their best interest.

Now, let's see how observant you were. Did you realize that the bold
typed first letter in each of the five questions spelled wants? That is
important. You need to determine what your wants are from your selling
career, then write them down. If you don't know what your wants are,
how will you know when you have achieved them? We will talk more
about wants and goals in Chapter 10.

Business Qualification Questions

Now that you have analyzed what your personal wants are, it is important you qualify yourself in the business of selling. Ask yourself the following questions, beginning each question with "HAVE I...

1. Searched for and studied all the necessary information about my
product or service? This is the first step in being properly prepared. You
are greatly hindering your chances for success if you are lazy at this point
in your career. The more time you spend studying your offering, the less
worry you will experience when you meet your prospect. It's also a good
idea to know your competitor's offering. You will see in Chapter Five,
Addressing Customer Concerns, how knowing your competition will help
you to feel confident of your product's strengths, and you will be able to
answer customer objections about your product's possible weaknesses.
If you don't know all you can about what your product or service can do
for the customer and how it compares to the competition, you'll never be a
success in selling.

2. Adopted a positive, respectful, and friendly attitude? I'm sure you
will agree with me, we would all rather do business with people who have
these qualities. It is important to remember though, the emphasis of this
book--quiet power. Remember you act like a lamb. Any lion-like ten-
dencies should remain within, quiet. Some people think being friendly
and positive means the sort of rowdy greetings, or slap-on-the-back activities that have created the negative image most people have of salespeople
today.

3. <u>Learned all the best selling techniques available</u>? You are well on your way to answering this question positively, just by reading and studying the concepts presented in this book. However, it is an on-going process. The time to show the lion within--your mental toughness--is when it comes to your continuous pursuit of educating yourself. There are many selling methods and techniques you can learn, but I would caution you to choose your educators wisely. Avoid imitating techniques that will not lead you to success.

4. <u>Eliminated possible objections through the practice and drill of good selling skills</u>? You will achieve that smooth, calm manner if you practice these skills until they become almost second nature to you. People will soon say, "What a natural in sales." We know better, don't we?

5. <u>Sought out all the prospects who can benefit from my product or service</u>? You can't afford to sit back waiting for customers to come to you. Think of your selling career as a constant quest for offering new opportunities to established customers, and the tried and true opportunities to new prospects. This is where the lion part of sales comes in. You must be the aggressive hunter when finding prospects, and the gentle lamb when leading them to take advantage of your offering.

Now look again at the first letter in every question. What does it spell? <u>Sales</u>. If you qualify yourself before you do your customers, you will be ready to meet every challenge as a professional salesperson. Have you asked yourself what you <u>want</u> from your <u>sales</u> career? If so, now ask yourself if you are prepared to do what you know you should do. If you answered these two questions with a yes, you are now qualified to sell. So, mix these ingredients for success with an abundance of common sense, and you have the makings of a Champion. Here's a great little sentence to remember when you experience any doubts or setbacks in your selling career: If it is to be, it is up to me.

Likes and Dislikes

Many salespeople have a problem with their own likes and dislikes. They tend to only sell what they like, and mostly to the people they like.

Doing this severely limits their income. Your job is to enthusiastically sell what will benefit the customers whoever they may be. During the course of your selling career, you will have to work with some people that you won't particularly like. We discussed how to deal with several personality types in the last chapter. Remember, if you refuse to work with someone, you both lose. You lose the opportunity to make a sale and they lose by not having their needs satisfied. That person will simply get his or her needs filled by someone else. Keep your mind and your opportunities open.

Another challenge facing salespeople is having to learn not to prejudge people. Earlier, we mentioned a bit about body language. Well, whether we realize it or not, we all make some sort of judgment about people the moment we lay our eyes on them. We judge them based on their physical condition, their clothing, hairstyles and posture. In sales, this is a dangerous habit and one we should all consider breaking. We mentioned the danger of preconceived notions earlier in the book. If you are truly committed to becoming a professional, you must force yourself to look at every customer with a clear vision. Eliminate those preconceived notions before they start costing you money!

Let me give you an example. One Saturday, a couple pulled up outside the real estate office I was working in. They were driving a rather beat up truck and were dressed as if they had been doing some sort of heavy labor. Another agent in my office took one look at them and said, "Tom, you can have this one." He walked away, leaving me to talk with this somewhat unkempt couple.

As it turned out, they were looking for a fixer-upper property to invest in. They had made a business out of buying run down properties and applying their do-it-yourself abilities to turn those properties into desirable homes. They would then sell the homes for a tidy profit.

Well, I helped them find their next fixer-upper. A few months later, they came back to me to have me help them invest some of their profits into a luxurious home for themselves. Over the years, I sold them many fixer-uppers and resold those homes when they were remodeled. Had I pre-judged these people by their appearances, I may have been the one to walk away from what turned out to be a very lucrative opportunity.

The Art of Common Sense

Let's look at this subject in its most basic form. To do this, put yourself in the buyer's shoes. You want a good quality product or service, you want to own it at a fair price, and you want as little hassle as possible in the bargain. This sounds fair, doesn't it? Now ask yourself as a buyer, to achieve that goal, would you mind answering a few politely asked questions that would help you get there?

The answer should be easy. If the style is right, if you are treated with respect, and if the questions have some point (meaning reasonable and intelligent conclusions), you wouldn't mind answering them, would you?

To get permission from your prospects to ask qualifying questions, simply ask the following question in a professional, lamb-like manner: "Mr. and Mrs. Walker, would you be offended if I asked you a few questions that would help me to better serve your needs, and save you some time and possibly some money?" Is that a question that would upset you if you were looking for a product or service? It's that easy to start the qualifying process, yet thousands of salespeople try to make sales each day with no idea if the customer is qualified to buy, or if they're talking to the final decision maker. So they usually end up showing the wrong product or discussing the wrong service with a person who may not be qualified to buy even if they were interested.

In most cases, salespeople seem to be afraid of asking questions. They fear losing control when the customer is talking. The truth is just the opposite. Perhaps it would help if you think of it as a way to help your customer clarify their wants. It has been my experience that many customers enter into the buying process with an unclear vision of what they really need. They begin with the attitude of a 'researcher.' They have an interest in the item or service, but don't know enough about it yet to make a buying decision.

Except for the regular purchases of daily life, the average person has difficulty making decisions about owning anything without some help. We all have so many choices anymore that the decision-making process has become quite complex. The reason so many of us need help in making decisions is that we're all afraid of making bad ones. Indecision is a great destroyer of sales, and a drain on energy, don't you think?

As a professional salesperson, I want you to remember this: **People love to buy after they own**. The biggest challenge is getting past the indecision before they agree to own. That's where quiet power helps you to make the prospect feel like they already own it. So, be confident and create those confident feelings in your customers.

This goes right back to asking questions. How do you bring about confident feelings in your customers? By asking questions. When you ask questions that will help you discover your customers needs, you not only save yourself time and energy, you help the customer get a vivid picture of what his or her needs and desires really are. It is absolutely vital to gather the information that will bring about a higher level of service and save your time, as well as that of your customer. Set a goal to master the skills of great qualifiers. **It is not uncommon for a strong qualifier to have a closing ratio FIVE times greater than that of a poor qualifier**.

It is unfortunate that the average salesperson attributes the professional's higher sales ratios to natural talent or their lion-like, aggressive abilities when in many cases, it's their skill in asking lamb-like, inoffensive qualifying questions. To the untrained salesperson, there definitely appears to be an advantage on the part of the professional. In reality, the poor salesperson just doesn't have the facts and "hot buttons," learned through effective qualifying, to effectively consummate the sale. Every poor salesperson needs to understand, when it comes to consummating the sale -- what you don't know can kill you.

You may recall in Chapter One, I used Jack Nicklaus as an example of using all your selling tools to the fullest. Which club could Jack Nicklaus afford to be poorly skilled with and still have the incredible record that he has? The answer is still, "None". Sales is exactly the same, and I will cover that in this book over and over again. Whatever step of the sales sequence you are weak in, will dramatically affect your sales income.

I realize I am getting off the subject of qualifying a little bit, but please bear with me. I have saved many sales careers over my 25 plus years in sales, sales management and training. Many of these rescued careers were people who thought they were bad closers, when in truth they were just weak openers. Etch this into your brain:

You cannot say a few magic words at the end of a poor sales job and expect the buyer to reach for their money.

Qualifying is a very, very important strategy in the art of selling and is usually not given its due respect by the average salesperson. When you qualify your prospects, you won't be desperately "winging it" during the sales presentation and when you ask for the order. You'll be asking them to own something you both know they want and can afford.

Career Warning

More sales careers are cut short by poor qualifying skills than any other reason. Poor qualifying is also, in my opinion, responsible for most sales slumps. Lack of time spent qualifying shows a lack of respect for the customer. It's like saying, "I don't need to ask you any questions. I know what's best. Let me do the talking."

At times, we salespeople get too smart for our own good. We may brag that we know what the customer is going to say before they open their mouths. We tend to shortcut the rapport-building and qualification process then wonder why our sales are down. Never, never, never take shortcuts in qualifying!!

Qualifying Questions

Now that we have determined that professionals ask for the right to gather information, and then use that information with integrity, let's look at a few examples. Remember, to be successful, you must also find out how your customer feels about what they already have. This points you straight at the information you need to make the sale, or equally important, alerts you to the fact that you'll be wasting your time trying to sell to that particular prospect. Every product or service has its limitations: Trying to sell outside those limitations is a waste of irreplaceable time for you and the prospect.

To illustrate the point, let's say Ted is working at Champion Sports Car Sales. He's on the phone with Mr. Collins, who is thinking about replacing the custom Roadmaster Elite he's owned for three years with something more sporty.

Mr. Collins: "Ted, why don't you come over here and give me your opinion as to how much I could get for my Roadmaster Elite in today's resale market?"

Ted: "I'd like to do that, Mr. Collins. But first, may I ask how you got my name?"

Mr. Collins:	"Jim Clark works with me. He bought a Champion XP-1 Sports car last month. It sure is a great looking car."
Ted:	Yes, it is. I'm glad to hear Jim is happy with it. May I ask, what have you enjoyed most about your Roadmaster Elite?"
Mr. Collins:	"Well, I guess that would be its classic style and the ride. It rides so smoothly that you don't feel a bump in this car. But, it seems kind of slow and bulky compared to Jim's new sports car."

Now, make a statement that will either get a minor agreement or bring up an objection.

| **Ted**: | "Yes, I'll bet the ride is great, but these days, a sports car can provide you with comfort as well as speed." |
| **Mr. Collins**: | "Yeah, I'm excited about having something with more get-up-and-go. I'm just not positive I'll feel safe in a sports car. My Roadmaster is big and safe. It practically glides over the road. Small cars, quite frankly, scare me." |

Now Ted's found out what he needed to know before wasting Mr. Collins' time, as well as his own valuable selling time. Champion Sports Cars sells the finest sports cars made. Not the big safe cars. Sure, Ted could show him a car with the get-up and go he wants, but they are definitely smaller than Mr. Collins' Roadmaster. The cars Ted markets are precisely the type that Mr. Collins wouldn't be happy with if he bought one. After asking a few more questions, he's eliminated Mr. Collins as a prospect for his sports car offering.

| **Ted**: | "Mr. Collins, from what you're telling me, I think it would be safe to assume that you might not be comfortable with a small sports car." |
| **Mr. Collins**: | "I've been thinking about getting a sports car for the speed and image. I thought you might have something bigger and safer, but with a little more speed than my Roadmaster." |

Ted: "Mr. Collins, I really appreciate your calling me,
                     but we're not the right people to serve you. Our
                     XP-1 is a small car with a sporty ride. We don't
                     have larger models of sports cars. I know someone
                     who is the area's leading expert on classic roadsters.
                     Let me get your address and I'll have him send you
                     some information."

Then Ted sends Mr. Collins a thank you note and asks him to remember Ted's name if he hears of anyone who is interested in owning a top-of-the-line sports car. This next step is most critical in increasing Ted's future business. He can't procrastinate. He must do what he said he would do for Mr. Collins.

Putting things off can often be a bigger problem than actually doing it. If it is impossible to act immediately, devise a system that will remind you of the things that must get done today. Remember, Ted has given Mr. Collins his word, and in sales your word is your reputation.

So, now Ted places a quick call to his business acquaintance who sells the kind of car Mr. Collins likes. When you establish a networking system like this one, other salespeople will feel obligated to return the favor. They will send you prospects who are interested in buying sports cars. Now Ted has developed two possible new sources of leads--those from Mr. Collins and those the roadster salesperson will send him.

Notice that Ted doesn't ask Mr. Collins to tell the other salesperson that he sent him. Instead he takes it on himself to call this non-competing member of the industry. Sure, it may take 15 minutes, but those 15 minutes can, in turn, bring back qualified buyers.

One more point, Ted will be sure to send a thank you note to Jim Clark for referring Mr. Collins to him. It's best for Ted to also tell him what happened. Hopefully, Jim will continue to tell others about his new car and someone he knows will want a small sporty car, too.

With the time saved by not trying to sell Mr. Collins' car, Ted continues taking and making calls. An hour later, he's talking to Max Michaels.

Ted: "What do you like most about your present car,
                     Mr. Michaels?"

Mr. Michaels: "It's a mover, Ted. It gets me where I'm going
                     fast."

Ted:	"Your car does 0 to 60 in about seven seconds, doesn't it?"
Mr. Michaels:	"Seven seconds? No way. But it's good for an easy 8 1/2 seconds, it's fast."
Ted:	"The Lightning Bolt will take you from 0 to 60 in six seconds."
Mr. Michaels:	"Six seconds! Wow!"
Ted:	"Mr. Michaels, when can we get you behind the wheel of the new Lightning Bolt to try it out? Would tomorrow morning or afternoon be best?"

If Ted had rushed out to see Mr. Collins' roadster, he would have missed Mr. Michaels' call. Someone else around the office would have given that test-drive and probably sold him a Lightning Bolt. On the other hand, he didn't just brush Mr. Collins off either. He might have a friend or relative who would be interested in a Lightning Bolt. Always take the time to send a thank you note with a few of your business cards. A future referral is more than worth the time.

You see, by qualifying Mr. Collins Ted saved time for both himself and Mr. Collins. Try not to waste your time working with people who want what you don't have to offer. If you waste time that way, you might have the "bad luck" to be out every time real business comes in.

Write Right!

One of the most important points in this whole book is this: **Never, never, never talk with a prospect without taking notes!** If you fail to take good notes on their responses to your qualifying questions, you may have to ask the same question again further into your presentation. Believe me, repeating yourself does little to instill confidence in your ability as a salesperson. Being able to refer to your notes and refresh your memory on what 's already been discussed will simplify your job and insure accuracy in all of your sales presentations and in all follow-up and service situations. I know I've said this several times and I might say it again -- don't wing it! Write it!

A Word of Caution

Now is a good time to caution you about qualifying over the telephone. Be careful that you don't over qualify on the phone. The most productive use of the phone is to use it primarily for making appointments. Remember, a lot of products can't be sold over the phone. If that's the case with your product or service, keep the goal of making an appointment in mind during all telephone contacts. That is the purpose of the phone contact -- to get an appointment for a face-to-face presentation. What you do sell on the phone is opportunity to present your offering. So, keep your qualifying questions to a minimum when talking on the phone. Ask just enough qualifiers to determine what you need to know to prepare an effective presentation. Depending on what you are selling, your first meeting might be a fact-finding mission. If that's the case, let them know. Instead of selling your product or service, you would be selling them on the fact that you need more information to properly help them.

I have recommended that you make up a checklist of everything you need to know to determine whether or not your product or service is right for each prospect you meet. Include all of your qualifying questions in that checklist. Fill in the answers to those you can comfortably ask over the telephone. Then, note those you still need answered during your appointment.

Good qualifying is one of the basics of selling that cannot be overlooked or sloughed off. Don't set yourself up for failure. Work on your style and questions then watch your income, and your base of happy customers begin to build.

Customer Needs or N.E.A.D.S.

The average salesperson today either lets the consumer totally make the decision as to what they want, or they try to steer the person to what that salesperson likes best. You will remember, we have agreed both of these approaches are wrong. Because of this, I've developed an acronym to help you remember key qualification questions. Picture in your mind the word needs, but spell it this way -- N.E.A.D.S. I know my spelling is a bit creative, but it will help you to think of meeting the needs of your customers. If you could get everyone in the company saying to themselves when they meet a customer, "I am concerned about their NEADS. I will discover the customers true needs and lead them to the right product or service for them." And in satisfying NEADS, you are then going to achieve a higher degree of accomplishment in your business.

So, let's take the acronym, N-E-A-D-S. The N stands for the word
Now -- 'What does the customer have now?' What is the reason for asking this? Most Americans, average consumers, don't make drastic
changes in their buying habits so, if you know what they have now, it
gives you a good idea of the type of people they are.

For example, we know that past experiences often dictate future decisions. So you need to explore the customer's past experiences. You want
to know what they have now so that in your mind's eye, you can see the
type of buying decisions they will make in the future.

Let's look at the second letter in the word NEADS. The E stands for
Enjoy. It is important to know what your customers enjoy about what
they have now. What was the major motivation for getting involved in
their existing product or service? Questions have to be structured to
enable us to discover their past. There is a good chance that what they
enjoyed about the product or service in the past, what they enjoy about
what they already have--they'll want again. This is usually true, unless
you can demonstrate a benefit in your product or service that is even better than the one they enjoyed when they purchased their present product
or service.

Now for the A. A stands for **Alter**. What would they like to alter or
improve about what they have now? We have talked about how constant
change is. Change is a potent force in business. In some ways, we are all
looking for change. More benefit. More satisfaction. More comfort.
This is why you want to develop questions to find out what your customers would like to change. What would they like different? Then you
structure your presentations to show customers how your company can
provide their desired changes in product or service.

After everything said about the D word, you must know by now that
stands for **Decision**. Specifically, who will be making the final decision
on the sale? Many times we meet someone who is looking for a car, a
stereo, maybe some furniture, and there is only one person. Is it wise to
assume they will be the decision-maker? Never assume anything about
your customers. They may be 'scouting' or 'researching' and will bring a
spouse or parent in later when it's time to make the final decision. Ask
qualifying questions to discover the truth. Many times the salesperson

who has not properly qualified the prospect will go too far in the presentation before finding out the real decision-maker is not present. You'll be doing nothing more than practicing your presentation with non-decision-makers. Wouldn't you rather give your best to someone who can truly benefit from your product or service?

Looking at the word NEADS, the acronym, we see that we have now talked about the following:

1. What the prospect has **now**.
2. What the prospect would **enjoy** having.
3. What would they **alter** about what they have now.
4. Who is the **decision-maker**.

But, what about the S--the last letter in the word NEADS? What do you think the S stands for? Think for just a minute. Some of you may be thinking, "Sale." No, that's not the word I am looking for. You and I are in the business of creating **Solution**s. We are in the Solution business. You see, we find out what the prospects need then we come up with a solution. In most cases, the solution is that they own the benefits of our products or services. I hope the material in this book helps you to find many successful solutions.

At my seminars one of the phrases I ask people to learn and adapt to their product or service is this, "As a representative of (name of your company) it's my job to analyze your needs and do my best to come up with a solution to satisfy those needs so you can enjoy the benefits that you are looking for." We serve consumers by finding out what they need and then creating the right solution. When we do this, we create a win-win relationship where people want to do business with our company. They give us business and, in turn, we both grow and prosper.

QUALIFICATION STEPS APPLY TO EVEN THE MOST UNUSUAL PRODUCT OR SERVICE

Let's take a look at how to ask the proper qualifying questions while finding out the needs of the customers. You work for the Champion Bird

Bath Company and your prospects are Bill and Helen, who're interested in possibly getting a bird bath for their yard.

Step #1   What do they have now?

Salesperson: "I want to thank you for letting me come in and talk to you. I'm glad that we enjoy a similar interest-- birds. I noticed you were throwing crumbs to attract birds. Do you also have a way of attracting them to a bird bathing system?"

Helen: "Not really. We just throw around a few seeds and we also hang a cake pan from a post to catch rain water so they can bathe."

Step #2   What do they like most about what they have now?

Salesperson: "That's great. Tell me, what do you like most about the way the cake pan bath works?

Bill: "Probably that it attracts lots of different birds and since we put that up, we always seem to have a large number of birds in the garden."

Salesperson: "I see."

Now the point is to keep digging for information. As long as they are showing interest, keep asking questions. This is where all your practice and drilling comes into play. When you know how you want to phrase the words you want to say, you won't experience those awkward pauses throughout the presentation. If you have not done your homework, your customers will be aware of it too. The unfortunate thing is, many times when customers hear you pause or stumble over your words they think you are either ignorant of your product or service, or that you are about to tell them something they don't want to hear. These awkward pauses often trigger fear or uncertainty. Either way, you have almost killed the opportunity to succeed.

If you pause in your presentation, make it a planned, purposeful pause. There are times when this is necessary. We will talk about that in Chapter Seven on consummating the sale. So, keep asking the questions that capture the customer's interest.

Step #3 What would you alter or improve about your existing product or service?

Salesperson: "Tell me, if you were to consider improving or altering your present system, what do you think you'd change?"

Helen: "Well, I would make it bigger. The big birds crowd into that cake pan and it's hard for the smaller ones to get near it."

Bill: "Yes, and I would make it shallower and lower so we can see them better while they're splashing around."

Salesperson: "That's why you throw seeds and built that little bath, because you enjoy watching them, isn't that right?"

Bill: "Yes. On Sundays we eat breakfast on the patio and we enjoy watching them."

Step #4 Who other than yourself will be making the decision?

Salesperson: "Tell me, and I know we're just discussing this, but if you decided to acquire a new type of bird bathing system, is there anyone else, other than yourselves, who would be involved in making the decision?"

Helen: "We would both make that decision."

Salesperson: "I see."

Pay close attention to the critical Steps #5 and #6.

Step #5 The triplicate of choice for product or service

Before I show you an example of triplicate of choice, let me tell you a bit about how it works. I have often tested the theory of triplicate of choice in my seminars, and it rarely fails to show that when given a group of numbers, such as, 1, 2, 3, and 4, statistics show that approximately 8% pick #1 while approximately 68% pick #3. You may be asking yourself why. I don't pretend to understand why, I have just found this to be true. I suggest you try it with your friends and fellow salespeople to prove to yourself how often it rings true. People will choose the middle number 68% of the time.

The important thing about this theory is not why it is true, but that it definitely is true. So, you don't have to understand it, you just have to learn to use the theory to help make you successful. This is how you let the triplicate of choice work for you. When you want to put statistics on your side, put the best offering in the middle of the choices you give your customers. Sure enough, about 68% of the time the customer will choose the middle figure.

Another way to use this if you are concerned about getting a "price objection" later in your presentation is to make the lowest figure the one you actually want them to invest. Then, if they do like so many people and choose the middle number, they can't come back later and say that the lower investment is too much.

If you want to use this method for choice of product, elect the product or service you have determined is best for the customer, put it in the middle of the choices offered, and there it goes again--68% of the time the customer will choose the middle offering. The offering you intended for them to choose all along. The following example will help you to get a clearer picture of the triplicate of choice. I think they'll most likely want the Wet Wings model.

Salesperson:	"We at Champion Bird Baths are very excited about our bird bathing systems. We have three types available. We have what we call the Birdy Bathette, which is a 20" diameter bathing system. We also have the Wet Wings, which is a larger 25" diameter. Then we have the Super Spa, which is a full 30" diameter, for the true bird lovers who would like to attract larger birds and greater numbers of smaller birds. Now, can you tell me which of these you think would best suit your needs?"
Helen:	"Well, the Birdy Bathette sounds cute, but I think the Wet Wings would be what we need."

Bill:	"Honey, we are NOT buying a bird bath."
Helen:	"Why? We've been saying for months that we needed to get something a bit more attractive for the birds. Which one did you like?"
Bill:	"Well, if we were to buy a bird bath, I would have to agree that Wet Wings is probably what we would want, but I don't think we really need one."
Salesperson:	"I see. By the way, do you know that Wet Wings comes in Parakeet Blue, Canary Yellow, and Swan White. Which color do you think would look best in your garden?"
Helen:	"Oh, I think the Swan White would look great!"
Bill:	"If we were interested, I think I would like the Parakeet Blue."
Helen:	"But Swan White is a classic. White looks so nice against the greenery and the patio furniture we bought last year is white."
Bill:	"Okay, you're right. Swan White would look best. If we were going to buy one, it would be Swan White."

Step #6   The triplicate of choice for money.

I'm using this to eliminate a money objection later on in my presentation. Read on and see how it works.

Salesperson:	"You know, because of green lawns and all the many different colors of flowering shrubs, Swan White is our most popular color. Our bird bathing systems appeal to many different types of people. Many people invest as much as $100. Then we have the fortunate few who can invest as much as $150 to $200. And then, we have those who are on a limited budget that cannot go higher than $75. Tell me, which group would you fit into?"

Helen :	"I would say that if we invested in a bird bath system, we would be in the middle category, $100."
Bill:	"Honey, we are not spending $100 for a bird bath!"
Helen:	"Well, if we're going to get one, I want the 25" so we can see them."
Bill:	"One hundred dollars for a bird bath?"
Helen:	"I think if we decide to do this, we should go ahead and spend the difference between the smaller $75 bath and the $100 bath, which is what we really need."
Salesperson:	"Bill, I see your concern. But you know what's exciting? The medium 25", Wet Wings in Swan White, right now, is available at a special investment of only $75."
Bill:	"Really? Well, that's good news!"
Helen:	"Wonderful!"
Salesperson:	"That answers your concerns, doesn't it? With your approval right here, you'll be enjoying that bird bath system by this weekend."

I hope you saw, through this example, that proper qualifying through questions can be so helpful to you. Helen did as so many people would. She chose the middle dollar figure. That choice told the salesperson they couldn't object to the lower investment. Did you also notice how the salesperson chose when to remain silent and let Helen assist him in the sale. She often overcame Bill's objections. If you are working with two prospects, it is beneficial to allow this to happen. Remember: If you say it, they can doubt you. If they say it, they must believe it to be true.

Now I know this example was almost comical. But that's fine. You should be able to have fun while you learn. Just think, if these questions work in this example, how much more effective it can be for your product or service.   You'll gain the greatest benefit from now taking the qualification questions and customizing them to your product or service. Use your imagination and make the material truly fit you and your product.

QUALIFICATION QUESTIONS

Let's look at an example of how we use qualification questions in the sales training industry. When a company is interested in sales training for their people, our qualification process goes something like this:

1. How are you familiar with our company?

If they were referred by someone, this is good information to know; it helps to establish a common ground. If Joe Smith referred our company to them, later we can give an example of how Joe Smith benefits from our product.

2. What type of business are you involved in?

This question helps us to determine which of our products will best serve the needs of the prospect. We also need this information because much of our material is customized to specific industries.

Another benefit to asking this question is that it may trigger names of other companies in the same industry that have benefited from the training. These companies could even be their competition. You can bet, if the competition has suddenly increased their market share, and that increase could be attributed in part to our training, that's a powerful illustration of the impact of how further sales training can give one the competitive edge.

3. How many salespeople do you have working with you?

We ask this question to determine which type of product would be best for them. If we know the number of salespeople is rather large, we know the importance of suggesting video training or a discount on a multiple order of books or tapes. Also, we can use this information later in the Reduction to Ridiculous decision-making method. See Chapter 7.

4. What is your position with the company?

If the prospect answers, "Owner" we would say: "Would you have a sales manager implement the training, or do you fill that position yourself?"

If the prospect answers, "Manager" we would say: "Who other than yourself would be involved in making a final decision?" We want to know if an owner, V.P., or some other administrator needs to approve the investment.

5. What type of training are you currently using with your salespeople?

If they are using training developed in-house, we have to assume egos may be involved in making a change. In other words, treat the subject carefully. Be lamb-like.

6. How was the decision made to own what you have now?

It could be that whoever made the decision to implement the training now used would also be responsible for making the decision to use our training. It doesn't hurt, at this point, to stroke their egos a bit. We let them know that we are sure that much thought, research, and hard work went into their current training program. Then we remind them of the personal recognition received for a job well done, and remind them of how terrific it would be to make yet another good decision that would benefit them as well as their company.

7. We have materials available on goal setting, personal motivation and sales management as well. Are you interested in researching a well-rounded training system at this time, or do you just want to focus on sales training?

We ask this after confirmed interest in our basic training program. Then once we have the final agreement on the basic training, we can recommend items for further consideration as an add-on to the original sale.

Let's look at a real estate example:

You work for Elite Real Estate and are working to help Greg and Barbara find a new home.

Salesperson: "Greg, Barbara, thank you for taking the time
                        to meet with me today. Would you be offended if,
                        in order to serve you better and perhaps save you

some time and money, I asked you a few simple questions before we go look at the home you called on?"

Barbara: "No, not at all."

Salesperson: "Greg, Barbara, can you tell me what type of home you have now?"

Greg: "Sure, it's a wonderful Tudor style home. We've lived there for two years and we love it, but I'm afraid we're about to bust out of it. We need some more room."

Salesperson: "Tell me, do you own or rent the home you're in now?"

Barbara: "We're renting, but our lease is up soon and we've been wanting to own a home."

Salesperson: "Can you tell me what you like most about the home you have now?"

Barbara: "I love that it has a big, wonderful backyard. Someone put a lot of work into that yard before we moved in. I like that the kitchen is in the back of the house so I can keep an eye on the kids while I'm cooking."

Salesperson: "That's great. How about you Greg?"

Greg: "Well, we get a lot of use out of the finished basement, and I like the fireplace in the family room."

Salesperson: "Terrific. Now, can you tell me what you would alter or improve on your present home?"

Greg: "We have three bedrooms; we really need four, or even five. Also, I would connect the dining room to the kitchen so on special occasions we aren't always carrying hot dishes across the front hallway."

Barbara: "I would have the back door moved to come into the laundry room so the kids wouldn't bring in dirt through the family room. Then, I would turn the garage so it doesn't face the street. It's always such a mess."

Salesperson:	"Greg, Barbara, if we are fortunate enough to find a home that will best suit your needs today, who other than yourselves would be involved in the final decision?"
Barbara:	"Greg and I, but we would have to make sure the children liked the home too."
Salesperson:	"What ages are the children?"
Greg:	"Tommy is 11, Susan is 9 and Barry is 6."
Salesperson:	"I see. Then you'll be concerned about the schools and recreational facilities in the neighborhood, right?"
Barbara:	"Oh, yes. We want the children to be able to walk to school if at all possible."
Salesperson:	"Alright. Not to be personal, but to do a better job for you, how much of your savings did you wish to invest in your new home?" (When asking a personal question, soften its impact by saying, "Not to be personal." This keeps you acting like a lamb so you can sell like a lion.)
Barbara:	"Well, we do have some money saved for the down payment. It would depend on the home."
Salesperson:	"What price range have you been considering? (Pause) Better yet, since most people today are more concerned with the monthly investment, how much do you feel you could comfortably invest each month in your new home?"
Greg:	"Well, we don't want to go much higher than $1,100 a month."
Salesperson:	"That's fine. If we are fortunate enough to find the right home today, will you be in a position to make a decision to proceed?"
Barbara:	"I don't know that we'll decide today, but if we find the right home, we certainly would want to get things rolling quickly."
Salesperson:	"Do you have a specific date in mind for getting moved into your new home?"

This will help you determine just how hot a buyer they really are. If they pick a date that's six months out, you know they'll want to keep looking until they find the perfect home or run out of time.

Once the prospect's have decided on a particular home, use the triplicate of choice to determine what initial investment they are prepared to make.

Salesperson: "When we are fortunate to find a beautiful home like this, we find some folks are prepared to make an initial investment of 15%. Then we have the fortunate few who can make an initial investment of 20 to 25%. Then there are those on somewhat of a limited budget and can only make an investment of 10%. Tell me, which group would you be in?"

Remember, the figure you are after is always the middle number, not in the sequence, but numerically. Very few people want to be in the bottom group, or the 10% group. Most people don't want to go as high as the 20-25% group. Studies have shown that given three figures, most people will go with the middle figure, or in this case, 15%.

Take the questions we've given here and re-write them for your product or service. See how many qualification questions you can come up with. Then, write them again in the order of importance. In other words, list the questions first that most quickly weed out those people who may not be qualified for your offering. The whole idea behind qualifying is to help you more quickly determine if you are talking with someone who needs, wants and has the authority to make a decision to own your product or service. Once you know they are the decision-maker and a good candidate for your product or service, the balance of your qualification questions will help you direct your presentation to tell them of the specific benefits and features of your product or service that they will want to own. Practice, drill and rehearse the questions you write until you can deliver them all with lamb-like warmth, sincerity and in the most courteous manner possible.

I've told you before and I want to stress it again: It doesn't matter what your product or service is. If you follow proven, step-by-step strategies and tailor them to your offering, they will work for you. You will become a 'natural' and you'll be on your way to becoming a true Champion!

Always remember questioning is your best opportunity to build rapport and show your concern for their needs. Use your confident, low key approach. Your customers will appreciate your style and professionalism.

CHAPTER 5
ADDRESSING CUSTOMER CONCERNS

Until you learn how to address customer concerns you're not going to come close to your highest earning potential in sales.

What I found in my selling career was that the hardest customers to sell were really those who had no objections at all, or at least didn't voice them. Many didn't voice their objections because they either had no means or no intention of buying. And, the people who did voice objections often ended up being clients. That's when I decided to take a different attitude about objections. You should, too. The next time you hear an objection look at it as a necessary step in a successful selling cycle.

What do customers tell you when they voice objections? They may be telling you, "Hey, I'm interested, but I need more information. Help me make a decision." After all, why would a customer object to something that is of no interest to them? I think you'll agree with me that most people don't spend time making objections to a salesperson just for the sake of debate.

If you have properly prepared for your presentation by qualifying your prospects, you realize their need for your offering even if, at first, they do not. The success of your presentation is dependent upon your ability to motivate and relate to the customer. This is not the time to throw your arms in the air and say, "Well, I give up. It's their loss." You have invested too much research, too much energy, and come too close to success to quit now. Yet surprisingly enough, many average salespeople do exactly that. You may be asking, "Don't sales pros ever quit?" Yes, they do. They quit being **defeated** by objections. Top salespeople think of objections much differently than the average salesperson. They think of objections as opportunities for prospects to learn more about what they are offering. Objections or concerns then become necessary steps in building to a successful consummation.

How the Untrained Salesperson Addresses Concerns

Let's take a look at how an average salesperson handles objections. As you follow this dialogue, see if you have fine tuned your hearing to recognize what went wrong. What can you find that almost guarantees most untrained salespeople an unsuccessful close?

Al is a carpet salesman for Everyone's Carpet. Because Al is not a student of selling, he has no vision for success. He is still making the same old pitch to Bob and Laurie that has worked about 20-25% of the time he has told it to other customers. Did you catch the lion-like words? When Al thinks about his initial customer contact, he thinks of it in terms of pitch, not presentation. He has never learned the skill of proper questioning. Why? Because Al is too busy telling instead of asking. The following dialogue proves my point. Make a list of the things you think Al is doing wrong.

Al: "Hi folks. (Shakes hands vigorously.) Glad to meet you, and welcome to Everyone's Carpet. Is there anything I can show you tonight?"

Bob: "We're just looking."

Al: "Well, make yourself at home. How about a nice Berber carpet? We're selling a lot of it these days so I can get you a good price."

Laurie: "No thanks. We're really just looking."

Al: "Oh, okay. (He moves back for a while, but soon he is by their side once again.) Yes, that's a beautiful piece of carpet. Bet that would look good in your living room. You know, you folks, sure look familiar to me. Did I sell you carpet before?"

Bob:	(By this time Bob is getting a bit annoyed, but Al fails to read his body language.) "No, I'm sure you haven't. We've never been in this store before."
Al:	"I've worked in several stores in the area. Where did you buy your last carpet?"
Laurie:	"We've never bought carpet before."
Al:	"Well here. I'll just follow you around a bit in case you need me. Not everyone is a carpet expert you know." (Now Al pauses trying to think of what to say next. He feels it's important to fill every moment with conversation.) "So, have you been looking for carpet long?"
Laurie:	"No, not long."
Al:	"Well, we've got the best. I've been selling carpet for over 20 years. I've sold a lot of people in all those years. (Now Al tries to point out his qualifications.)
Bob:	(Disgustedly walks away)
Laurie:	"We'd really just like to look around on our own. Maybe we could take one of your cards."
Al:	(He digs a card out of his jacket pocket.) "Here you go. How much carpet do you need?"
Laurie:	"We're not sure exactly what we're going to do at this point."
Al:	"You folks seem pretty sensible. How about a nice brown, heavy duty carpet. It's great for young couples. It won't show any stains from all the kid's spills and traffic."
Bob:	"The carpet is for my mother."
Al:	"Well, do you think she'd like the brown?"
Laurie:	"To be honest with you, we are looking for Bob's mother to give her an idea of who has the best prices. So, we have no intention of buying carpet until she comes with us."
Al:	"We are the cheapest in town."
Bob:	(He has had enough and is heading for the door.)
Laurie:	"Maybe we'll be back."
Al:	"OK. Bring your mom in to see me. I can give her a good deal."

As soon as Bob and Laurie are out the door, Al turns to another salesperson on the floor and says, "They'll be back. I know I sold them on the
fact that we have the cheapest prices in town."

Okay, look at your list of things Al could have done differently. How
many mistakes did you find? Your list should look something like this:

1. From the very start, Al entered into the encounter with a lion-like
pitch (there's that dirty five letter word again) that only worked, at best,
25% of the time. He did not vary his style or message. Before Al can act
like a professional salesperson, he must learn to think like one.

2. Al put himself, and his expertise, before the customers' needs. He
forgot to make them the stars. He never even asked for their names.

3. Al did not practice **calm** enthusiasm. Instead he was too boister-
ous, aggressive, and impolite to bother to find out the customers' needs.

4. He asked poor questions -- things that were irrelevant to the sale.
No tie-downs or tag-ons.

5. He specifically did not ask leading or discovery questions to gather
information.

6. Al forgot a major question. Who would be making the final decision on the carpet?

7. Al was lost when it came to handling objections. He told the customers instead of asking.

8. Because of his selfishness, Al failed to involve Bob and Laurie in
the presentation.

9. Lastly, you have to wonder if Al will ever improve his skills if he
fails to face the reality of his situation -- he needs professional selling
skills if he wants to do better.

Congratulate yourself if you recognized most of the mistakes Al
made. It's a funny thing, but after you have begun to educate yourself on
the techniques of successful selling, you will more readily recognize poor
salesmanship. It is amazing how those like Al ever make any sales. You
may not think anyone could be as bad as Al and that we exaggerated in
this role play. Believe me, once you start listening to and watching other
presentations, you'll be surprised to find out how many thousands of

"Al's" are out there. Now look again. Were there any mistakes you didn't catch? A good exercise would be for you to rewrite this conversation, turning Average Al into a Champion using the questioning techniques from Chapter 2 and the N.E.A.D.S. formula from Chapter 4.

How the Professional Salesperson Addresses Concerns

As a professional salesperson, you must smile inside when you hear an objection, because you are now ready to go to work. Until you learn how to address their concerns, you cannot achieve your potential in sales. To give the greatest amount of service to your customer, you must be able to help them get all the information they need to put their fears to rest.

Here is how we teach the professional to do it:

1. Hear them out
2. Feed the objection back
3. Question the objection
4. Answer the objection
5. Confirm the answer
6. Attempt minor close
7. If minor close receives a positive response, move toward finalizing the sale.

We'll elaborate on this system in a moment.

Please highlight and imprint this statement on your brain:

**OBJECTIONS ARE NOTHING MORE THAN
THE RUNGS UP THE LADDER
TO CONSUMMATING THE SALE**

The only way to climb this ladder is to grasp and overcome the rungs called objections. Unless you face them, grasp them, and reach above them, you'll never reach the top and become a true Champion.

If you've been dreading or avoiding hearing objections, perhaps you haven't learned the fundamentals for handling them. Before we get into that, let's define our terms. Overcome objections or address concerns, in a spirit of education, not one of battle. You are not out to prove yourself victorious. You are an educator, a provider of information to your customers so they can make wise buying decisions.

What is an Objection?

An objection is a statement by your prospect that he or she wants or needs to know more. If the objections your prospect voices are really requests for more information, they are a required ingredient in the selling recipe.

Actually, the more uncomfortable and insecure prospects feel, the more likely they are to raise objections. Unless they have conditions that prohibit the sale, raising objections can often be a way for them to say, "Hey, take it slower. I need some time to think." What's happening here is that his or her emotions are taking over. This person wants what you are offering, however, the logical side of them is telling them to be more cautious -- to think this thing through. Please realize this is a normal aspect of any selling situation. Because of this discomfort, many times objections don't come at you sounding like polite requests for more information. But as a professional, you realize this and you know just what to do about it.

If you are sensitive to the customers' objections, slowing down the pace will allow you to build a more secure relationship. Approach your presentation hoping for objections--hoping for an opportunity to dispel your prospect's fears. In doing this, each rung of the ladder will be strong and able to support the next objection or help you reach a successful culmination of the sale.

There are two types of objections, minor and major. Keep this in mind: **MINOR OBJECTIONS ARE DEFENSE MECHANISMS**.

As I said before, usually a minor objection will tell you that the prospect is trying to slow things down. This doesn't mean that they don't want to buy; they are simply looking for time to think before committing themselves. As we saw in our Bird Bath qualification sequence, many times when working with couples, one spouse will bring up an objection and the other spouse (who is very interested) will handle it for you.

Of course, not all objections can or should be overcome. Some can be bypassed when first heard and handled later. Others can be totally ignored.

What is a Condition?

A condition is a valid reason for not going ahead. It's an objection that may be difficult, if not impossible, to overcome during this meeting, but don't let that stop you from trying again at another time when the condition might be surmountable. You will often encounter conditions that will prevent the purchase. What was the condition in the example of Al? Good, you were paying attention. Bob and Laurie were not the ones who would be making the final decision.

The most common condition for large investments is lack of money, no credit, or bad credit. No matter how great the opportunity may be, if the prospect can't afford it, there may be no point in wasting your valuable selling time with them. (But before you ever get into a presentation that might generate objections, you already know the prospect is qualified, right?)

Remember Mr. Collins' desire to own a new car in the previous chapter? He called Ted because he wanted a new car, but by further questioning Mr. Collins, Ted soon discovered he was up against a condition. His company did not carry the style of car Mr. Collins wanted. Because Ted practiced proper qualification techniques, he quickly recognized Mr. Collins' objections for what they really were--conditions. He then referred the customer to someone better able to meet Mr. Collins' needs.

Ted epitomized the true professional. He was trained to recognize conditions. This is the main purpose of qualifying your prospects: <u>To determine whether there are any conditions that will make the final agreement impossible</u>. Champions don't waste the prospect's time trying to overcome impossible conditions. Instead the professional salesperson lets the customer know they are available for consultation or can be contacted if needed in the future. They help the prospect to save face if a condition surfaces. They show genuine concern, even if it means taking a few minutes to put them in touch with someone else who could better serve their needs. And, don't forget the most important step, send a thank you note and ask for the referral. The professional salesperson carefully backs down the ladder leaving it in place for future use.

Even skilled qualifiers may occasionally be well into their selling sequence and then encounter what appears to be a condition. If this happens, treat it like an objection; try to break it down. Use the steps we'll cover in this chapter. If you can't break it down, it's a condition -- a valid reason for not going ahead.

This is what separates the educated professionals from those who think if they just continue to talk, they will eventually overcome any condition. Sometimes the most professional selling in the world cannot overcome conditions, but you can be sure ramming your product or service down their throats doesn't sell at all. That lion-like approach will only exhaust and frustrate both you and your prospects. You are expending precious energy that could be used more productively with a properly qualified prospect. It is time to be realistic. Many salespeople have a problem letting go. Take advice from the professionals, or learn it later from your own experience. It can be pointless to keep going when you come up against a condition that you can't meet. Don't become so emotionally involved that you lose your ability to see the difference between an objection (which can be overcome) and a condition (which cannot).

For example, remember when Al was trying to sell carpet to Bob and Laurie? If Al would have bothered to ask qualifying questions, he would have recognized a condition existed that prevented the sale from taking place just then. They were looking for carpet for someone else, and that someone needed to be present to make the final decision.

Now look at the difference between how Al handled the condition during his carpet offering, and how Mr. Collins' condition of not wanting a sports car was taken care of. Because Mr. Collins was qualified by a professional salesperson, his objection was quickly identified as a condition. You must not only recognize a condition when you come against one, but you must make the most of the condition. Since you can no longer hope to consummate the sale, do the next best thing--refer the customer to another professional who will return the favor. Never underestimate the benefits of networking.

Remember: **A condition is a valid reason for not going ahead**. Please be aware that many conditions you will encounter in your selling career may be only temporary. So, when you first hear a condition, be certain to ask questions about it. It could be the prospect doesn't have any money just now, but has a tax refund coming. Perhaps they're waiting to sell their other car outright before investing in a new one. Always remember that circumstances may change. A Champion salesperson learns just what the circumstances are before deciding whether or not they can overcome a condition.

An objection is a request for more information. If no conditions exist and they don't buy, you may not have done your job.

If you represent a fine quality product or service, and you have presented it with skill and integrity, you may not have done your job well if the customer didn't buy. When people own your product or service they benefit, don't they? So, let them. Do your job. You need to act like a lamb, but you've got to have the selling instincts and drive of a lion. Lambs that aren't lion-hearted allow themselves to be led astray. Selling means helping people benefit and grow. Many mediocre salespeople get blown away at the slightest breeze of an objection, letting the opportunity sail away with it.

I hope you will make the decision today to buckle down and not get blown away. Start today to take the material in this book and put your energies into learning the skills. Soon you'll be going into a presentation ready and willing to hear the noes, so you can utilize your professional selling skills to get to a yes.

TWO DON'TS AND ONE DO THAT CHAMPIONS LIVE BY

Please highlight these three precepts so you can review them quickly and often.

1. <u>Don't argue.</u> Do you know how many salespeople will argue with a prospect? The prospect voices an objection, and the salesperson runs him or her over with anger, sarcasm, or some other form of sales-killing pressure tactic, trying to bypass, ignore or bury the objection. Don't be like a lion going for the throat. If you go in for the kill, you'll find that when the dust settles what you've killed is your chance of ever doing business with this person again.

By arguing, you become trapped in a no-win situation. Face facts. You cannot argue a customer to your point of view. You can, however, adopt **quiet** power and use the persuasive selling skills and techniques that have been presented to you in this book to lead them. If the prospects think your product or service is not right for them now, they may change their minds at a later date. So do what you know you should do. If the objection becomes a condition, let go of it. Remember to follow up with a thank you note and ask for possible referrals.

2. <u>Don't attack prospects when you begin to overcome their objections</u>. Put space between your prospects and their objections. Develop sensitivity to what your prospects are feeling when they voice an objection. Show compassion for their concerns, not fiery determination to prove them wrong. Nobody wants to be proven wrong. You can't make sales by winning battles of logic and losing the war of emotions.

For example, look at this conversation between a car salesperson and their customer:

Salesperson:	"Well, you've been looking at this car a long time, and you've certainly asked a lot of questions. When can I put you in the driver's seat?"
Customer:	(As the customer bends to take a closer look at the paint.) "Well, the paint..."
Salesperson:	(Doesn't give the customer time to complete what he thinks is an objection.) "It's true, we have had some problems with the paint in the past, but we have worked hard to correct the problem."
Customer:	"Oh, you've had a problem with the paint? I was just going to say how much I liked the color."

By jumping the objection, or what the salesperson thought was going to be an objection, a problem was created where none existed before. Now the customer is thinking about the quality of the paint because the salesperson was sensitive to a closer inspection. Listen and learn from the customer's objections.

Objections should tell you many things. They can tell you where the prospect's interests lie. They can also tell you what you should emphasize, eliminate, or change before the prospect will agree to buy. Lastly, objections can be the feedback you need to effectively lead the prospect to a positive final agreement. What you should not let objections do is discourage you from offering your product or service.

    3. <u>Do lead prospects to answer their own objections</u>. A sales professional always tries to steer the prospect to answer their own objection. Why? Because, as I explained earlier: **When you say it, they tend to doubt it. When they say it, it's true**. A pro works to develop skill at this. Most of the time, the prospect will answer their own objections if you give them time and ask the right questions.

    Many buyers have certain reflexes and they don't even realize that they come out as objections. If someone tells you, "I only see vendors on Thursday," or someone comes into your store and says any of the following: "I'm just looking." "I want to shop around." "I want to sleep on it." "We'll get back to you," you're hearing reflex objections.

Six Steps to Handling Objections
    We listed these earlier, but let's go into a deeper explanation of them.

    1. <u>Hear them out</u>.
    Don't interrupt. <u>Many untrained salespeople leap on an objection before the prospect has a chance to even finish voicing it</u>. The objection is treated as if it were an alien that needs to be terminated before it grows or multiplies.

    So what happens? The prospect not only feels irritated, but pressured. Pressure is your worst enemy in professional sales. Another thing to remember is that by pouncing on the objection, you might have missed needed information. What happens to your credibility if you answer the wrong objection, or worse, bring up a new one? Don't ruin your chances of getting that yes. **Listening is your greatest tool**. Hear them out.

    There is something else to consider when you are tempted to immediately jump to defend or argue an objection. You create a "me against them" power struggle. Then you stop responding to the prospect and begin reacting to the objection. If this happens, you are in danger of losing your dignity along with the sale. Soon you are asking yourself,

"What happened? I gave them my best and they rejected me." Prospects and their objections can only have as much power over your emotions as you give them. The key is to treat objections as little bumps on your otherwise smooth road to success. Remember, you and your customer are in this together. You are on the customer's side, not against them. Their concern is your concern. To look at an objection as an area of concern you must work on it together for a win/win outcome. Objections are not just something you must overcome for your benefit.

2. Feed the objection back.

The prospect tells you, "The freezer compartment on this is just too small."

You feed it back by saying, "So what you are telling me is that you need a bigger freezer compartment to accommodate your family, is that how you feel?" Sometimes feeding it back can get them to answer their own objections. Again, husband and wife buyers will often overcome the objection for each other when the trained salesperson uses this method. They have even been known to assist in finalizing the sale. For example, if the wife has just stated that the freezer compartment is too small, and you don't jump in too soon to defend your product, the husband might suggest they use the freezer in the old refrigerator in the garage as a storage unit. By being lamb-like, you have the advantage of letting the husband answer the objection. After all, who's the wife much more likely to believe or take advice from? If her husband suggests this solution, she will probably take it into consideration. Not only that, but you may now have the husband thinking positively about owning the product.

3. Question the objection.

Ask if it's really that important. There is no such thing as a dumb question. Ask them to elaborate on their objection. Ask them gently, with warmth and sincerity, "So that I may serve you better, may I ask...?" Avoid any hint of sarcasm, impatience, or annoyance. If you let them get into details, they might remove the objection themselves. While the prospect tells you what he or she is feeling, you have more time and gain more information to examine how you might suggest solving it.

4. <u>Answer the objection</u>.

I can tell you now that throughout your career, no matter what you sell, your product or service will have a few weaknesses you will wish it didn't have. Things the competition might offer that your company doesn't. Don't dwell on this. Move past it.

A Champion studies the weak points their offering has and learns how to handle the situation. They often do this by admitting the disadvantage and then immediately comparing it to an advantage. "Yes, our cargo beds are about a foot shorter, but they are 25% deeper than any other model. This is because our studies have proven that..."

A real talented professional even learns to brag about the objection. Some even use it as a selling tool. One of the stories about just such a situation is one that happened when I was in real estate. I had a very nice house available for sale. Unfortunately, across the street was a home that looked like a disaster. The landscaping was practically non-existent. There was a car up on blocks in the driveway. In general, the home was a real eyesore. No one could sell the nicer home because of it.

I had a buyer contact me who specifically wanted a home in that neighborhood. I knew that particular property was just what they were looking for. To overcome the challenge of the eyesore across the street, I found out how long those people had been living there. It was four years. At that time the average family moved every three years, so it was a good bet that these people, too, would consider moving in the near future. When I pulled up in front of the home, I pointed out the eyesore to the prospective buyers. I didn't wait for them to bring it up. I told them about the odds that those people would be moving in the near future and surely whoever purchased the home would be able to get it at a low market value and would fix it up. Meanwhile, the house they wanted would also sell for a lower investment because of the eyesore. In the long run, they stood to gain as the value of their home would increase when the other home was fixed up. They agreed with me and took advantage of the opportunity.

This is a prime example of the principle of bragging about an objection. The key is to find a way to turn the objection into an advantage or at least offset any negativity the objection might bring about.

5. <u>Confirm the answer</u>.

Don't respond to the objection and then leave it hanging. The prospect may not have understood what you said. Or maybe they stopped listening before you covered the point because they were thinking of something else. After you've answered the objection and you feel that you did resolve it, confirm it. Say things like:

* "That clarifies that point, don't you agree?"
* "That is the answer you're looking for, isn't it?"
* "Now, with that question out of the way, we can go ahead."
* "Now that settles that matter, doesn't it?"
* "If you agree with that, we can move on."

6. <u>Change gears - "By the way..." and ask another question</u>.

Your objection answer has been confirmed, now immediately move on. To let the prospect know that the last step is over, and to move on to the next step, make an appropriate gesture. Some things you might do are to look or step in a new direction, turn the page in your proposal, or shift in your chair, mark something on your paper work. Make some kind of physical move. Wave your hand. Use body language as your tool. As you do this, move on to the next step by saying, "By the way..." and ask another question.

Remember, you must learn and practice this method. Adapt it to your product, service or area, and know it like the back of your hand.

Always be sure to watch your prospects carefully during any objection-handling situation. You don't want to push them into going past an objection if you haven't truly covered it. Their body language will tell you whether or not they're satisfied with your answer. If you ignore that and move on, you'll be doing nothing more than sweeping the objection under the carpet. It won't be gone. It'll very likely re-surface later.

It could happen that they are embarrassed to tell you they don't understand what you said when you thought you handled the objection so smoothly. Instead of going ahead with the sale, they head for the door and you never learn the real reason why you didn't make the sale.

When you kill an objection, you want to make certain it's dead and not kill the sale along with it.

Four Essentials For Handling Objections
Here are four ways to help you overcome specific barriers:

Objection Solver #1. - <u>Put the shoe on the prospect's foot</u>.

It's common in sales, especially when you are just starting out, to take over an established territory. Let's suppose that is what you are doing. Within a few days you find out that the salesperson before you didn't leave the position because of the great job they were doing. Now you are left to pick up the pieces and deal with a lot of unhappy people.

Use this to overcome a direct challenge arising from a possible negative experience with your company. For example, you work for National Medical Supplies. You sell medical supplies from bandages to state-of-the-art diagnostic equipment. You've just arrived at the office of Scott Mitchell. You no sooner pull your business card out of your pocket when you run into trouble. Mr. Mitchell says, "Thanks for coming, but we bought an EKG machine from your company two years ago. It broke down after a year, and I couldn't get that clown who used to come here to do anything about it. I don't want whatever you're here for. So, if you'll excuse me..."

The first thing to do is to preface your first sentence with two of the most difficult words to say. "I'm sorry." These words are two of the most seldom spoken, yet most highly effective words in our vocabulary. Practice them. Don't worry about being right or wrong. You really had nothing to do with it and the customer knows it. By admitting you feel badly about what happened, you diminish his anger, while answering his objection. It takes a strong individual to say, "I'm sorry."

Next the Champion immediately puts the shoe on the prospect's foot by saying, "I'm sorry Mr. Mitchell. I understand that you had a problem in the past with getting the service you deserved. Let's pretend for a moment that you're the president of National Medical Supplies, and you just found out about a sales representative who was side-stepping our service agreements. What would you do?"

Wait for his answer. It will probably be one of two things: "I'd fire that person." Or, "I'd move them to a different department where they didn't have to work with customers." After you have listened to their whole answer--letting them get it all off their minds, say, "As you can see by my presence here, he/she is no longer servicing your account. We understand that we will have to work very hard to regain your trust and confidence. You have my commitment, as well as that of the president of National Medical Supplies, to give you the first rate service you deserve."

Don't get into lengthy explanations. Don't keep any discussion of past disasters alive. Keep in mind what you feed becomes the strongest influence on your thoughts and actions. If you focus on the negative, your prospect will too--he or she will continue to think about the raw deal received from the previous salesperson. Move right into your presentation. Begin by speaking about the wonderful, exciting things you and your company have to offer.

If the prospect still displays an obvious annoyance to you at this point, end the meeting. Remain respectful, polite and friendly at all times. Be sure to leave the door open for a possible later contact. To do this let them know that you are in agreement with them and you feel your company owes them. If you see them begin to soften, you may want to ask one more time for an opportunity to make it up to them. Be sympathetic. Let the customer know you understand how they feel and send them a thank you note for taking the time to see you and discuss the matter.

Remember, time heals all wounds. The Champion salesperson is courteously persistent in situations like this. By proving your professionalism, you'll soon win them over.

Objection Solver #2. - <u>Change their base</u>.

Ask a question that highlights major benefits while it dwarfs minor objections. Parents have this step down pat. They have learned the art of distraction. If their child gets fussy because they cannot have exactly what they want, parents substitute another object. They present the substitution as something much more desirable. Many times the child forgets what they wanted to begin with and reaches for the exciting new item. What have they done? They have emotionally involved the child with their offering.

Professional salespeople must do much the same thing. When your customers begin to hedge because of a perceived weakness your product or service may have, you must practice the art of distraction. Draw their attention from the weakness and focus on the product or service's strengths. Allow the customer to see that what seems important to them, just now, may not amount to much in the overall scheme of things. It may actually be very minor. Take a look at the following example from car sales:

You've shown the car and the prospects like it. But as you're walking with them to your office, the husband suddenly starts fighting you.

Prospect: "The trunk is too small."

You: "Just to clarify my thinking, how much too small do you feel the trunk is?"

Prospect: "I'm not sure. It just looks small."

As you feed it back, elaborate on it to see whether it's more like a condition than an objection. Remember, a condition is a valid reason for them not to go ahead. When they tell you, you'll know what you have to work with.

You: "It's really about an average size trunk for this size car. Let me make sure I am understanding you correctly. In other words, you don't feel you have enough trunk space for the things you normally carry with you, is that how you feel?

Prospect: "Well, not completely, but I do think it's small."

At this point, if the wife doesn't jump in and overcome the objection for you, change his base.

You: "Tell me Mr. Miller, and this is an important question sir, because your answer can eliminate this car from consideration, what will you base your decision on--the size of the trunk or the high performance engine with the luxury interior you said was important to you when we first began talking?"

Prospect: "Well, I really want luxury and performance."

In most cases, the benefits they want will outweigh their concerns about the size of the trunk and you'll be able to move on toward the final consummation.

If they're primarily concerned about the size of the trunk, you now have a situation where your product doesn't qualify for a definite need that must be satisfied. He will then have to make a big choice and will need your help. You'd better suggest he forget that car and find one that better suits his needs. And, don't forget one of the most important points. Be very lamb-like at this point. When you ask these questions, be careful not to be offensive. Even though you may be asking what seem like ridiculous questions, ask them in all sincerity. Let the customers know that if this really is a great concern of theirs, then it certainly needs to be considered.

Here's another example. You're with a prospect who is considering your home exercise equipment.

Prospect: "One of my major concerns is that I'd really like to have a machine that gives me a good workout and doesn't have lots of extras that I don't need."

You: "Many of our customers tell us as they rapidly achieve a higher level of fitness, they get great benefit from the added features. (You ask cordially) "Mrs. Kerrigan, what will you base your decision on, the four or five extra weights and crossbars, or the opportunity to improve your physical condition in the privacy of your own home?" Here is where you want to repeat back to the customer all the added features your product offers, at no extra cost to the consumer.

Prospect: "Improve my physical condition."

Then you eliminate the objection by saying:

You: "This model costs the same as other models without some of these features, and if you ever sell it, you will get a much higher return for the extras. As you become more fit you might be glad that you have the extras at no additional cost."

Objection Solver #3. - The guarantee.

The prospects walk into your retail store and settles by one of your home entertainment centers. When they ask questions, you give your demonstration and learn two things: They are Mr. and Mrs. Kelly, and they want that entertainment center. After qualifying and demonstrating your product, you go through a few test closes with no success, and then Mr. Kelly says, "Thanks for your time. We'll think about it and let you know."

What does "I'll let you know," really mean in cases like this? It usually means, "Now that I've found what I want, I'm going to shop around and see if I can find it any cheaper."

Remember the rule. Always lead them toward answering their own objections. Here's how it goes:

Prospect: "We'll look around and get back to you."

You: "Fine. That's a wise decision. Mr. Kelly, would you be offended if I ask you a couple of questions that might save you both time and money before you leave? Were you impressed with the quality of the picture and sound of this entertainment center?"

Prospect: "Oh yes."

You: "Is the console the size you're looking for?"

Prospect: "Well, yeah. It's about right."

You: "And you mentioned that you wanted a programmable CD player, but not something too elaborate. Does this model fit your needs on this?"

Gently list all the things they were pleased with that you have written in your notes. As you do this, work in very briefly, all the positive things you can that they initially elaborated on. Remind them that you service everything you sell. You have free delivery and installation. Oh, and don't forget to mention the liberal credit terms. In some cases, you'll be able to help them own the entertainment center they want by striking a responsive chord with some of the services that you can offer. If not, you'll be able to get down to the final objection, which is usually money. When you get them to agree that the reason they won't buy is money, you've isolated your problem.

Most people want to shop for the best price once they know what yours is. In some businesses, it's common practice to agree to match any other price on the identical product they can find within 30 days. This often gets the prospect to commit to making the purchase, intending to look around further but being able to enjoy its use now. This is a very low-risk proposition since once the customer owns your product or service they tend to move their focus toward other more pressing business. However, they are often impressed by this additional service consideration.

You might say something like this, "We could have you enjoying this beautiful home entertainment center within 24 hours and still assure you that as you shop around, we'll match any lower price you might find on this identical unit. Our customers love this guarantee and I must admit every once in awhile even as low as our prices are, we must match a lower one. We're happy to do it, though, because we know you want the lowest price, with the least amount of hassle. Should I set up a morning or after-noon delivery for you?"

Objection Solver #4. - Review their history.

This method is especially effective if your product or service is some-thing that is bought on a regular, on-going basis by organizations. You might be selling industrial raw materials, professional services, supply items, or some generic merchandise. The buying of these products or ser-vices often becomes a matter of habit. It's easier to keep on buying the same thing from the same source than it is to cope with change. Do a lit-tle investigating. Find out who made the decision to change from what was used to what is being used at the present. If it was the decision of those you are presenting to, remind them of the possibility of benefiting when they are again able to either save their company money or help it operate more efficiently.

Speaking of change, there is something you should know about it. Change is probably one of the few constants in our world, yet many peo-ple fear or resist it. Are you one of these people? Do your customers fear change? If so, you need to encourage them to take advantage of all the opportunities that your product or service will bring them. The Champion makes change sound like an adventure. It really can have the excitement and surprises of an adventure. It's good to remind your customer of the history of good service you and your company have provided, but you cannot live in the past. The business world is ever changing and you must become knowledgeable about current consumer needs so you can properly service them.

The bottom line is to value your old customers and treat them with as much enthusiasm and energy as you give to your new customers. Many salespeople don't really keep on their toes with their established cus-tomers. They usually put more value on acquiring new business than on keeping the business they have worked so hard to establish, even though the cost of acquiring new customers almost always far exceeds the cost of keeping the old ones.

Of course, many successful salespeople become overly satisfied with their positions and get careless. When you stop bringing fresh ideas to established customers and stop keeping in close touch, a gap begins to open between giving the best service possible and what you are actually giving. The wider the gap grows, the more likely it is that your competition will discover it and try to fill it.

When you have established customers, keep in close personal touch with them. Be sure to keep them posted on any new developments in your industry, and always be looking out for their best interests.

WINNING CUSTOMERS OVER FROM YOUR COMPETITION

This strategy gives you another avenue to gain new prospects--from the competitor's old customers that have been neglected or taken for granted. Here's how you convince them they need to consider change:

You're selling service, print advertising space to be exact. Your magazine is Champions Monthly. So Smooth Soap, a major advertiser, buys all their advertising from Sales, Inc., a competing publication. You are going for the business in a meeting with Melanie Holton, So Smooth's advertising manager. (With many products or services, you'd have to ask what they're using now. In this case, you know because you read the competing publications to see who is advertising in them.) You are already one step toward success--you are entering into the meeting prepared.

You: "Are you satisfied with Sales, Inc., Mrs. Holton?"

Prospect: "Yes, we are. They have done a wonderful job for us."

Remember to be attentive to the prospects unspoken language, as well as what is being said. You take a look at her body language. She is sitting on the edge of her chair, which may indicate to you she expects this meeting to be short. She has her arms crossed in front of her. This might mean she is blocking what it is you have to say. Now take a look at her face. Most people wear their feelings on their faces, and you can know what they might be thinking if you are observant. Look at her lips. Are they tight, or are they relaxed in a pleasant smile? In this case, Mrs. Holton's lips are somewhat tight, showing her slight annoyance at having her busy schedule interrupted.

Having observed all this, you know to adopt a somewhat brisk, businesslike message or style. Get to the point soon or you will lose her polite attention. If you spend 20 minutes making pleasant conversation, she will most likely decide you're wasting her time and close her mind to your offering. If her body language and tone were more relaxed--sitting back in her chair, smiling, saying, "Yes, the ad we're running in Sales, Inc. is doing well for us," then continue. She put the emphasis on the ad rather than the magazine. She's already open to a presentation and it might be worthwhile to spend a little more time building rapport.

For now though, we have to face a sterner prospect. You can't worry about rapport-building. You need to earn the right to give your presentation at all. Here's how you do just that.

Let your customer set the tone, then be flexible enough, and prepared enough to go with the flow. Okay, you know what you're up against, so now you get down to business. You begin to get permission to present a wonderful opportunity that is beneficial to Mrs. Holton and her company.

You: "How long have you been using Sales, Inc.?"
Prospect: "About three years."
You: "And before Sales, Inc., did you do any print advertising?"
Prospect: "Yes, So Smooth started in Sold Monthly in the late eighties."
You: "May I ask how long you've been So Smooth's advertising manager?"
Prospect: "I've been here for over five years."
You: "Then I'd probably be safe in thinking that you had a great deal to do with the switch from Sold Monthly to Sales, Inc."

Now you have your prospect emotionally involved. When you begin to talk about the part Mrs. Holton plays, she automatically perks her ears to hear what you are getting at. Have you ever noticed how people like to talk about themselves, or how they like others to recognize their accomplishments? Although it is important to remember not to let yourself be intimidated by your prospects, you had better come prepared with everything you've got when you meet a prospect like Mrs. Holton. Now let's see what is happening in the presentation:

Prospect: "Yes, I did."

You: "And you made that switch based on quite a bit of research and analysis, didn't you?"

Prospect: "Yes, we did quite a bit of research. We made a detailed market analysis of three publications and felt that Sales, Inc. would generate more buyers for our advertising dollars."

You: "You were looking for sales potential when you did your study three years ago, weren't you?"

Prospect: "Absolutely."

You: "And the results have lived up to your expectations?"

Prospect: "Yes. We have been very satisfied with the results."

You: "Tell me, since you received greater performance by considering and then making a change three years ago, why would you want to deny yourself the opportunity to repeat the process? (Don't pause.) Your research back then led to greater profits for So Smooth and greater professional prestige for you. (Now you really have her emotionally involved. You have just pointed out what's in this for her personally.) You did it once, so the possibility must exist that you can do it again. Do you feel this could be true?"

Now take a look at her body language. She is now sitting back in her chair with her arms resting comfortably in her lap. The expression on her face is no longer slightly aggravated, but instead it is thoughtful.

Prospect: "Yes. It's a possibility."

You: "Wonderful. It'll just take me a few minutes to explore that possibility."

She's given you the right to make your presentation. The last change worked out well, and she wants to look good to management. So now she has logical and emotional reasons to consider another change. Notice how this questioning style was concise and businesslike. Very well-planned and methodical. The salesperson captured Mrs. Holton's attention by being aware and respectful of her busy schedule, by being observant, and by being flexible with the message and style. Now that has the makings of a professional.

I hope you can see the importance of being adaptable. Keep your product or service in mind, rehearse a number of variations so that you'll roll it off smoothly no matter what they say. Instead of going back to your manager and saying, "So Smooth's happy with Sales, Inc. They wouldn't even talk to me." You'll go back to your manager with the order.

Learn the pattern. Write out your presentation or questioning sequence, then practice it. The next time someone says to you, "We're happy with what we're buying now," you'll think to yourself, "You may be using them now, but within the hour, you're going to get happily involved with me."

The job of the Champion is to realize that he or she represents the finest product or service available, and then to make sure that everyone who can benefit from it owns it. After you get Mrs. Holton and So Smooth switched to Champions Monthly, after you do a thorough job of follow-up and great service, Mrs. Holton will be delighted that she made the change. We both know it couldn't have happened unless you learned and applied the essentials for addressing customer concerns.

If all else fails, try this question to determine what their true objection is: "If price were no object, what would you want this product or service to do for you that we haven't already discussed?"

Practice the objection handling steps on your family, your friends, etc. The art of handling and overcoming objections smoothly is a way of thinking. Anyone can learn these steps; it just takes practice. The job of a Champion is to realize that he or she represents the finest product or service available, and then to try to find everyone who can benefit from it, to own it.

Adapt, practice, and use these techniques and you'll be well on your way to becoming the number one salesperson in your organization. Now that's exciting, isn't it?

Objections or areas of concern are your friends. The more of them you can solve for your customers, the most delighted they will be with your service.

CHAPTER 6
THE POWER OF WORDS
AND SPEECH

We have talked about words and the pictures they create in our minds, as well as in the minds of our customers. I want you to stop for a moment and think about the power you have in the proper use of language. Now, let me ask you this: Do you use that power to your greatest advantage?

Each word in the English language represents a symbol or picture in our minds. When we hear the word, we picture a symbol of what that word represents. We have emotions attached to each of those symbols. As an example, let's consider these words, SPRING, SUMMER, AUTUMN, WINTER. Depending on your particular experience, each of those words can generate positive or negative emotions in you, right?

The same applies to the words you use in your contacts with customers. You don't know in advance which words will generate positive feelings in your clients about you, your product and your company. That's why people in selling must become extra sensitive to the use of words if they want to have successful careers or businesses.

There are many words common to sales and selling situations that have the potential of generating fearful, lion-like images in the minds of our clients. From my experience and that of hundreds of thousands of other salespeople, we have found it extremely valuable to replace those words with more positive, pacifying, lamb-like words and phrases.

For example, one of the most commonly used words in sales is the term **contract**. What type of mental image does that term bring to your mind especially when you picture yourself as a consumer? For most of us, it's negative. We have an image of fine print, legalities and being locked into something that requires legal action to get out of. For that reason, I recommend that salespeople stop using that term, unless your particular line of business requires it. Instead, use the terms **paperwork, agreement** or **form**. Think about each of those terms for a moment. Do they bring to mind threatening images? If they do, I'll bet those images are a lot less threatening than those created by the term **contract**. Do yourself a favor and eliminate that term from your vocabulary. Use **paperwork, agreement** or **form** instead.

I know this sounds like a small thing, but having a successful sales career is little more than a string of small successes that add up. You can make major blunders and lose a sale, but I believe more sales are lost when you add up the small things that get you a NO. Making the most of the little things is nothing more than developing good habits. Good habits are very important to a pro. They leave nothing to chance. The details you start letting slide today will come back to haunt you sooner than you think. That is why we teach basics. These seven steps are a foundation you can go back to each year like pre-season camp for professional athletes. The pros always take time to re-learn the little things. No one in the universe gets off course faster than we humans, so be sure to take the time to get the little things right.

What about the terms **cost** and **price**? What pictures do they bring to your mind? If you're like me, I see my hard-earned cash leaving my pocket. That's why I teach salespeople to substitute the terms **investment** or **amount** in place of **cost** or **price**. When most people hear **investment**, they envision getting a return on their money which is something positive. Now, there are products for which the term **investment** would not be appropriate so let's use the term **amount** for them. That word has been proven to be less threatening to most consumers than the terms **cost** and **price**.

The same idea goes for the next terms, **down payment** and **monthly payment**. Most people envision **down payments** as large deposits that lock them into many smaller **monthly payments** for a considerable time period. They may see themselves receiving bills and writing checks every month. Not too positive a picture, is it? Replace those phrases with these: **initial investment** or **initial amount** and **monthly investment** or **monthly amount**.

What about the term **buy**? For me, there goes my money out of my pocket again. Let's use the term **own** instead. **Own** brings to mind images of where I'm placing the product in my home, showing it with pride to friends or relatives, and many other positive thoughts.

The next lion-like terms I'd recommend you change are **sell** and **sold**. Many salespeople will tell prospective customers about how many units of their product they have **sold**. Or, they'll brag about having **sold** the same product to another customer. What are the mental images here? No one likes the idea of or the feeling derived from being **sold** anything. It sounds as if the customer didn't really have much say in the matter. Replace **sell** or **sold** with **helped them acquire** or **got them involved**. Those phrases create more lamb-like images of the salesperson being helpful and the customer being involved in the process. Customer involvement indicates their willingness to go ahead.

Another term that I feel is over-used by salespeople is the term **deal**. What does this bring to mind? Something we've always wanted, but never found. Top salespeople never offer **deals** to their clients. They offer **opportunities** or **get them involved** in **transactions**.

Customers don't raise objections about our products or services. They express **areas of concern**. We don't have **problems** with our sales, we may, however, have some **challenges** with our **transactions**.

We never **pitch** our product or service to the customer. We give them professional **presentations** or **demonstrations**.

As authorities or experts on our products or services, we don't earn **commissions**, either. We do, however, receive **fees for service**. If a customer ever asks you about your **commission** on a sale, I'd like you to consider using this phraseology: "Mr. Johnson, I'm fortunate that my company has included a fee for service in every transaction. In that way, I am compensated for the high level of service I give to each and every client, and that's what you really want, isn't it?"

The last, but definitely not the least important, lion-like term I recommend you change is **sign**. If you do nothing else, please make this change. Never again ask a customer to **sign** your **agreement, form** or **paperwork**. What happens to us emotionally when we are asked to sign something? In most cases, a warning goes off in our heads. We become very hesitant, cautious, wanting to take time to review whatever it is we're signing, looking for the infamous 'fine print.' We've all had it drilled into us from early childhood never to **sign** anything without careful consideration, haven't we? So, why would you want to create that emotion in anyone you were trying to **get happily involved** in your product or service? Instead of asking them to **sign**, ask them to **approve, authorize, endorse** or **OK** your **paperwork, agreement** or **form**. Each of those terms is more lamb-like, asking instead of telling and more likely to result in a closed transaction.

As I said before, it may sound a bit foolish to you now to concentrate on such minor details, but some of those little details pack a hefty punch. When you have written down and practiced your own particular product close, go through it and make sure you have changed the wording to stress ownership from the prospect's perspective.

Trade Talk

Another area regarding vocabulary that we must consider is trade talk. This involves the use of words and phrases that are particular to your field of work. If you are selling medical supplies to doctors, you'd better know the trade talk and use it liberally. However, if you are selling stereo or computer equipment to the general public, limit your use of technical terms to the bare minimum.

You see, the human mind can only assimilate information rapidly if it understands what is being said. If you are talking to Joe Consumer about bits and bytes and he doesn't understand those terms, his mind will stop at those terms and try to find an image that fits closest to what he thinks it might be. For some people that may take awhile and they'll miss the next few valuable points you relay to them. In other words, you've lost them. If things begin to sound more complicated than he can comprehend, you will possibly squelch his desire to ever own a computer and completely lose the sale. More often than not, you'll simply lose the customer and a more lamb-like salesperson, who uses lay terms and simple definitions, will make a relatively easy sale to Joe within the next week or two when his desire to own a computer resurfaces.

Unlimited Vocabulary

Words are readily available to all who wish to control them. Webster didn't reserve certain words and their meanings for the rich. Everyone has access to the same dictionary. Everyone has the same opportunity to choose the words that make their speech outstanding and memorable. You have a choice of any one of millions of words to establish your meaning. So why aren't you more careful to choose your words properly? Knowing that your words reflect the person you are, don't you think it wise to investigate the choices you are making and why?

If everyone is influenced by words, then wouldn't you agree the professional salesperson should recognize and choose professional language? Take a look at the two following examples. Be aware of the differences in language. Even though you cannot see these two people, you will create a mind picture of each of them and their selling styles.

Mrs. Worth, manager of Continual Care Hair products, has been courting an account with a major chain of salons for two months. These salons now carry Mrs. Worth's competitors' product but have agreed to hear a presentation by one of her representatives. It is now up to Mrs. Worth to choose the salesperson who will be able to achieve a successful consummation to all her hard work. She calls a meeting with each salesperson she is considering. The one who succeeds in representing their company could receive a sizable increase in earnings. Which one will she choose? Which one would you choose?

Manager: "Now that you understand what will be expected of you, how would you give this presentation?"

Dawn: "I would just love the chance to tell Mr. Dunn (owner of the salons) how much better our products are than what he's using. I would go to Mr. Dunn's salon tomorrow morning. I know I could convince him to dump what he uses now and replace his stock with ours."

Manager: "What is your next step?"

Dawn: "Well, after I got all the information, I would tell Mr. Dunn what we could do for him and I would try to get him on my side before the presentation to his staff, so he could help me sell his stylists on the products."

Manager: "I'm interested to hear how you would do this, Dawn."

Dawn: "Well, I guess I'd tell him how much money he would save, and how much more he'll make by selling our products."

Now, here's the same conversation with Sue.

Manager: "Sue, now that you understand what will be expected of you, what would you do?"

Sue: "I believe the first step would be to contact Mr. Dunn and request a meeting at his convenience. Then, with your approval, I would examine your files on the salon, so I am prepared for the presentation."

Manager: "What is your next step?"

Sue: "I will ask Mr. Dunn to show me his salons. I will familiarize myself with Mr. Dunn's needs, his stylist's needs, and that of their clientele. Then I will offer Mr. Dunn the opportunity to use Continual Care Hair products and ask his permission to present the products to his stylists."

Manager: "How would you do this, Sue?"

Sue: "While it's important to consider the financial benefits, I will encourage Mr. Dunn to examine the improved condition of hair that has been treated with Continual Care products. This would result in happier customers for Mr. Dunn as well as increased profits. Would it be possible to take a few company models with me on the presentation, Mrs. Worth?"

So, do you get a picture of the two salespeople? It is obvious Mrs. Worth has also created a picture in her mind of which one will represent her company with the most success. I believe it to be Sue. Did you choose Sue also? What was most influential in making your decision? Was it Sue's **calm** enthusiasm? Was it her thoughtful manner? Go back and see if you can pin-point the turning point of Mrs. Worth's decision. It really began with Sue's word choice of "I will..." instead of indefinite terms. Sue begins to speak as if she has already been chosen, while Dawn is still saying "I would..." This is a subtle change in words but very effective. It isn't long before Mrs. Worth is agreeing to send models with Sue for her presentation. So, are you getting the picture? Aren't words powerful?

As I have been thinking about the power and importance of words, it has occurred to me to take a closer look at the word "close". The word "close" has become one that is giving customers and salespeople alike more and more misgivings. We have all been taught that you must "close the sale" and all you hear is **close, close, close**. Somehow the word doesn't relate to the lamb. It's more lion-like, isn't it? Because of this, I searched for a word that didn't seem so final--the end, not like a closed door. Who wants to be closed? The thought of being a "closer" sounds very aggressive to many people. I think it's a word that has kept many people out of sales. Nobody wants to be closed. It almost sounds as if you're doing something against your will. We know this is not true in professional selling, but closing is still not an attractive word, so I am going to change it.

From now on, I am going to use the word, **consummate**. I'm going to exercise my options by choosing a word from Webster's dictionary that is more suitable. This is how Webster defines the word consummate: "To raise to the highest degree, to perfect or complete." What a great phrase, "To **consummate** the sale!" It signals both an end and a beginning. An end to laying the foundation and the beginning of a potentially great, long term relationship.

Another benefit is the picture it puts in the mind of the salesperson. Consummate means to perfect, or complete. <u>Therefore, I hope this creates a picture in your mind of the end to a series of events, not just a close</u>. As we have discussed, selling is a series of well-orchestrated events not a slam-dunk, pat-yourself-on-the-back, it's all over, close. After all, when your customer becomes the owner of your product or service, isn't that the beginning of a mutually beneficial relationship --not the close?

Too many salespeople for too long have made too much of the word "close". As we discussed earlier, the close is just one step of the selling process, and if all other steps have been done correctly, it's not difficult to effectively consummate the sale. Simply stated, the close or consummation is the final step in the information-gathering and information delivery process that leads to a logical and emotional outcome. This outcome benefits both parties.

WHAT YOU SAY AND HOW YOU SAY IT

Sales is all about what you say and how you say it. You need both sides of the equation to reach your peak. You need to do both equally well. That is why we talk about quiet power to change the image of the 'talk-talk-talk' salesperson. Your quiet confident manner and tone is the key.

For the rest of this chapter we'll cover some areas of consummating sales. As we do this, say the words of the salesperson in all the examples in a quiet, sincere and confident manner. Don't overdo it. Be yourself. Remember, it's OK to express enthusiasm for the possibilities with your customer as long as you keep yourself under control and stay ready to listen to their responses (and watch their body language). Remember always, the customer is the star of every contact.

CONSUMMATION IS MORE THAN CLOSING

After all the information has been gathered, all concerns have been addressed, and the information delivered, we come to the moment when a buyer acts like any other typical buyer, ourselves included. We all are familiar with the, "Well, I don't know's," or the "We need to sleep on it's," or the, "I want to think it over's," or any one of 100 other stalls. If we all have experienced these feelings of doubt, how can we expect our customers not to have them? Even though we want the product or service, we are afraid to go ahead because we have to part with our money, and money is security.

For example, let's look at dollars as units of security with one security unit equaling one dollar. A car may cost 18,000 security units due in 36,

$500 security unit payments. This can be a frightening thought, even if you want that shiny red convertible so much you can't stand it. Our job as sales professionals is to help customers overcome feelings of fear and procrastination before the excitement wears off. If we didn't, very few people would make major purchases. To accomplish this 60% of the time, we use questions. The other 40% of the time we do it with assumptive statements, stories and a few other methods. The main purpose of the question is a test to see if they have made a decision to go ahead or if they still have some reservations.

For example:

1. "Will you be the only one to drive the car, or will you let your children drive it too?"
2. "Won't it be great having your own washer/dryer and not ever have to go to a laundromat again?"
3. "Can't you just picture your children playing on their new swingset?"
4. "Won't it be nice going to a restaurant or the theater and not worrying about your car because of this alarm system?"
5. "Who besides yourself will be enjoying the benefits of this stair step machine?"

Any answer to those five questions is valuable to you. The answers will let you know the customer's state of mind regarding your product or service. Let's take a look at the first three:

Product: Car - "Will you be the only one to drive the car, or will you let your children drive it too?"
1. They may say, "No, my insurance couldn't stand it. I would be the only driver." Notice the word "would" not "will". That could be the key word. "Would" might mean they don't have enough information for a decision. "Will" may mean you should ease into the consummation process. This is a good example of why it is imperative that you listen closely when your prospect is speaking.

Product: Washer/Dryer - "Won't it be great having your own washer/dryer and not ever have to go to a laundromat again?"

2. In this example, when you have qualified the prospects, they may have told you they are in the process of purchasing a new home. Later, you test question about the laundromat. Their response: "Yes, it will be great not to have to go to the laundromat, if our loan on the new house is approved."

Now you have conflicting signals. Yes, they want your product, but they don't have anywhere to put it right now, so this is where you must become creative.

Product: Swingset - "Can't you just picture your children playing on their new swingset?"

3. In this example the prospect might respond, "Yes, we are having a birthday party this weekend. Do you have a service that can set it up for us?" Again, I hope you will know what to do.

As you can see, these test questions have served two purposes:

1. To set you up for consummating the sale.
2. To pop an objection which lets you know you have more work to do.

What do all these questions do? They lead and discover. What other important element do you see in these questions? Each question is worded in the "here and now". This makes the question of ownership immediate for the customer. While creating a picture in their minds, be sure to place them in the picture. When the customer can imagine themselves owning your product or service, and they have even created a picture with them or their family using it, you have them emotionally involved. You have successfully appealed to their emotional wants.

You must create an emotional desire within your customers to own your product. You create this desire by first asking important leading and discovery questions. So now we are back to the questions again, but asking the proper questions is the buildup to a successful consummation.

ASSUMPTIVE STATEMENTS

An assumptive statement is a statement that assumes the prospect has already bought your product or service. If the customer goes along, they own it, at least mentally. All you have to do at this point is help them decide on delivery and method of investment.

Example: Computer

1. **Salesperson:** "Once we upgrade your computer system, it will be so easy for you to produce those higher quality forms that you said you wanted."

   Prospect: "That will be great. We've really needed to upgrade."

   Salesperson: "Would you like installation during business hours or would an evening when the system is down be better?"

Example: Swimming Pool

2. **Salesperson:** "All the kids in your neighborhood will love playing in your new pool."

   Prospect: "I'm probably going to have trouble getting my kids out of it."

   Salesperson: "When should we start digging? Would this Saturday or next Monday be better?"

WORD PICTURES

Let's take a moment to see if you are comprehending what I have been teaching. Did you notice anything wrong with the dialogue between the salesperson and the prospect in the above example? Look at what the salesperson said in Example #2. "All the kids in your neighborhood will love playing in your new pool."

Does that statement paint a mental picture that is desirable to everyone? Remember what was said about the power of words. It just takes a few careless words to destroy hours of work. Look at this example again.

Is there a chance that the prospect will think of a pack of children yelling, running, pushing each other in the pool, and in general just making their lives miserable? I'm not saying this is the case, but it's possible, so be careful. Wouldn't it be better to make a statement such as: "Most of our customers tell us they enjoy spending quality time with their families in their new pools."

Moving on to the salesperson's next statement: "When should we start digging? Would this Saturday or next Monday be better?" Again, be careful of the word pictures you are painting. The prospect might envision a huge tractor roaring through their yard digging up plants and enormous mounds of dirt making a big mess of the home, and on a weekend to boot.

Wouldn't it be better to say: "Some people prefer to be present when we begin the first phase of their new swimming pool, others prefer to just say "when" then have us tell them when the pool is ready to swim in. We can begin Phase One Saturday or next Monday which would you prefer?"

I can't emphasize enough how important your choice of words is to your selling career. Your words can make or break the sale without you even knowing it. In many cases, if you ask the customer why they didn't buy from you, they may not be able to put their finger on what it was. They just didn't feel right about going ahead. Remember, words create images, which bring about emotions, so start paying careful attention not only to your prospects, but to how what you say affects them.

If you use language that is acceptable and professional, you will be identified as a Champion by your peers in sales, your competitors, and your customers. When these people hear your name, they will picture a Champion, because you have created that image. How do you think much of that professional image was created? An overwhelming percentage of that image was created through choosing the words that identify you as a professional.

Just like others, you tend to judge or categorize people by the words they choose to represent them. For instance, if someone mumbles all the time or fails to make eye contact, what do you think about them? You would probably think they have a poor image of themselves. You might place them in a category of a person with little self-confidence. The assumptions you made about this individual would depend on how you categorized him or her.

Another point to consider is your accent. People in nearly every region of the United States have accents-- a certain way of saying particular words. These accents can be charming or irritating to others, depending on their existing assumptions. If you do business in several areas of the country, you are probably already aware of this.

For example, if you are from the South and must do business with folks in the Northeast, be prepared to talk a bit faster than your normal rate of speed to keep their attention. Also, you might want to train yourself to listen more effectively because people in that part of the country tend to talk faster than the people you are used to being around.

The opposite goes if you are a Northeasterner doing business with some Southerners or Californians. Some people from the South and on the West Coast handle business in a more relaxed manner than those in your part of the country.

Please understand this is not an exact science and each person you make contact with will be different, but the more prepared you are, the better your chances of making a favorable impression on those people you wish to have own your product or service.

Think of your words as little ambassadors. You employ them to go before you and create good will. Surround yourself with ambassadors determined to represent you in the best light possible. To do that, they must create positive images and pictures in the minds of others, so appoint your ambassadors well.

Take the time to make a list of powerful, but easy-to-understand words and phrases that are specific to your product or service. Then, test them on a friend or relative -- someone who is not a qualified prospect. If they don't have a clear understanding of the terms, prepare brief definitions of those terms in "lay" language. Then, the first time you use the terms with new or prospective clients, give them the definition.

Let's move on to Example #3 in our assumptive statements.

3. **Salesperson**:   "Once your new commercials go on-the-air, are you going to need assistance to handle all your new business?"

    Prospect: "Gosh, that would be great. I think we can handle just about anything with our current staff."

Salesperson:	"Would you want your spots to run in the morning, or would afternoon drive-time be better?"

4. | **Salesperson**: | "Your oriental rug is going to look great in the dining room." |
|---|---|
| **Prospect**: | "I was thinking it would look better in the family room." |
| **Salesperson**: | "Oh, you're right. That would look great. Shall I ask the seller if they will leave the brass wall lamps? They would go perfectly with your rug in the family room." |

5. | **Salesperson**: | "Your newly remodeled kitchen is going to bring more light into this whole area." |
|---|---|
| **Prospect**: | "I'll be so glad to get all that dark cherry wood out of there." |
| **Salesperson**: | "Shall we begin construction on the 5th or the 10th?" |

I would like to have you re-read the assumptive statements in numbers 3, 4, and 5 and see if you can create word pictures that are more desirable. For example, let's consider the salesperson's final statement in #5:

"Shall we begin construction on the 5th or the 10th?"

Did you notice that this statement was rather abrupt and lion-like? Soften it a bit by saying:

"Yes. I think the white oak you chose is fabulous. Do you mind if we get those measurements now? I will need to get them to my cabinet maker today so we can be sure they will be installed 30 days before Christmas, as you said you wanted." You should feed back what they liked and what they said they wanted, then ask to go ahead non-offensively. Feedback, now that's an interesting word. Let's go into further detail on feedback.

Feedback

Let's define feedback as it refers to sales. There is a certain knack to giving effective customer feedback. The professional doesn't just spit back all the positive things that could be said about the product or service, that would simply serve as an endlessly tedious list. When you have properly qualified your customer, you know what benefits you need to stress to get your customers happily involved with your offering. Sure you could go through and tell them every wonderful thing about your offering, but chances are you will bore them with unnecessary information that may be of little importance to them. So, when you feed back or repeat your product's strengths, be sure to emphasize those things you have discovered that will be of interest and benefit to your prospects. This will reinforce your movement toward a positive consummation, and that's what feedback is all about. It's a tool you can use to help give you strong (or reinforced) sales success.

Now that we have discovered feedback as a type of reinforcement, let's take a closer look to see just how it works. It can be effective when used both negatively and positively, but if you desire successful consummations to your sales you should most often focus on the positive feedback. The result of positive feedback can be evidenced all around you. When you are aware of the results of positive feedback, you will begin using it in your sales sequence.

Take a moment to examine all the many instances of how feedback works in your daily life. For example, when you compliment your spouse for losing those annoying ten pounds that have been making him or her feel negative and uncomfortable, they are more likely to want to keep the weight off. Even though they like the new thinner look, they also like the extra attention and praise they received when you recognized their effort. That little bit of reinforcement helped them to continue the difficult job of losing weight. The reinforcement you give your customers will encourage them to continue the difficult decision-making process. By practicing genuine reinforcement, you have established a strong measure of control and forward movement toward a successful consummation.

The same thing occurs in the workplace. When you give feedback to yourself and others who help you to accomplish your goals, you accomplish today's goals quicker, and encourage others to help you with tomorrow's tasks. The next logical step comes when you practice positive reinforcement with your customers. Here are some examples:

"That's a good question." Or, "That's a good point to consider." can be used when the prospect raises a question.

"You're picking this up quickly" can be used as part of your demonstration.

"It's obvious you've done your homework" is another good, positive statement.

Giving positive feedback and reinforcement can have long-lasting affects. Think of positive reinforcement as a means of verifying someone's worth. When you practice positive reinforcement with your customers, you are saying to them, "I value what you have to say."

I hope the message in this chapter reminds you for the rest of your selling career to choose your words carefully. If you do, I guarantee you'll achieve greater success.

CHAPTER 7
THE STORY OF CLOSING

Everyone loves a good story. The best stories are those that make the listener feel the events of the story can happen to them. They draw the listener in, making them able to see and feel from the perspective of the key players in the story. They become emotionally tied to someone or to some event in the story.

Where do the stories come from? Most stories come from your real life experiences or those of the people around you. And what you say to bring about a positive consummation to your sales process is nothing more than a story. You tell stories about others who have needs, interests or desires similar to those your current client has. The stories should help them feel they aren't the only ones to have ever faced a decision like this about your product or service.

Sales stories help people to overcome fear or procrastination or both in making ownership decisions. In the world of sales, these stories have been called "closes" for as long as I can remember, but in most cases, they are all just short stories. I will give you a few examples and you write down after each example what you feel that story is meant to overcome: fear, procrastination, or both. As a by-product they may also give a feeling of confidence to help the prospect make a decision now.

1. THE "FACT WEIGHING" SCALE APPROACH

This approach is used to help your prospects make a final decision when they say they need time to weigh the facts.

Here's an example of how to use this story with Kevin and Karen Smith in a real estate office:

Tom:	"Do you feel that the home on Third Street might be the best decision for your family?"
Kevin:	"Well Tom, that home is a pretty big investment. I don't know that I'm ready to make a decision on this right now."

We have asked a lot of questions up to this point and we are now ready to put the answers to work for us. I can see that he and Karen really don't want to make the final decision. They're impressed with the home. They need to get the family moved quickly. The numbers work out. They are trying to avoid committing. In other words, they are behaving like typical buyers. This is a perfect opportunity for the Fact Weighing Scale Approach.

Tom:	"Could it possibly be, Karen and Kevin, that the challenge is that you haven't had a chance to weigh the facts involved?"
Kevin:	"Yes. I think that we haven't really gotten to the heart of this thing yet."
Tom:	"I understand how you feel and weighing the facts before making a decision makes a lot of sense, don't you agree?"
Karen:	"I think that's probably true."
Tom:	" In fact, when I'm in this type of situation, I use a method called the "Fact Weighing Scale Approach." Here's how it works: First, I draw a scale. On the left side of the scale, I pile up, just like small weights, the reasons I feel it makes good sense to go ahead. On the right side of the scale, I pile up the reasons I feel are against it. Then I simply add up the reasons on each side, and see which decision is the best."

The important thing here is to keep going with the flow of the conversation, rather than try to rigidly stick with a set of words you've memorized and then spit out like a recording. Once you master the material you'll know how to weave it into any conversation.

Tom:	"So why don't we analyze the decision and get down to the heart of it, as you put it?"
Both:	"Okay, let's do that."

Tom: "Great. So, the reasons for the decision go on one side of the scale and all those against the decision go on the other side. Than we add each side up and the right decision will be clear. We have the time, haven't we? It will take just a couple of minutes."

Kevin: "Yeah, okay."

I have a long list of things they liked about the home because I made notes on every positive comment made since we drove into the neighborhood. If they run out of positives off the tops of their heads, I'll remind them of those on my list.

Tom: "Let's start it off here. Let's think of the reasons favoring the decision. You agree that the home has all the features you were looking for, isn't that right?"

Karen: "Yes, it does."

Tom: "And we've already established that with the right financing you could actually have a smaller monthly investment than on the home you are in now."

Both: "Right."

Tom: "You said you wanted to be close to the elementary school and this home is just three blocks away. That's certainly a plus, don't you think?"

Both: "Absolutely."

Tom: "Let's go on. You thought the professional landscaping in the backyard was impressive."

Karen: "Yeah, the kids would have a lot of fun in that yard."

Tom: "Wouldn't they? Let's write that down. And what about the outside of the home? When we first pulled up, Karen, remember how you got so excited?"

Karen: "It is a beautiful home."

Tom: "Let's see, that's five, can you think of any others?"

Kevin: "Well, we really liked the extras in the newly remodeled kitchen."

Tom: "All right, we'll put that down."

Kevin: "I like all the big trees on the property."

Tom: "Okay. We'll put that down too."

Karen: "Oh! We both liked the sunken bathtub in the master bedroom."

Tom: "Great. Is there anything else you can think of?"
NOTE: Set a goal for between six and ten items on the plus side. If you haven't reached ten at this point, refer to your notes and remind them of other items to add to this side. When that goal has been reached, continue with:

Tom: "Now, how many reasons can you come up with which may be against you purchasing the home?"

Kevin: "Well, let's see. The down payment is a concern. Until we sell the house we have now, it could be tough to come up with that kind of money."

Tom: "Okay, what else?"

Kevin: "We were really interested in finding a home that had solar heating."

Tom: "Those are both valid points Kevin, can you come up with any others?"

After a pause, it's obvious that Karen and Kevin aren't coming up with any more objections. I don't even have to answer those objections at this point, so I say:

Tom: "All right, why don't we just add up the weights?"

I show them the list and together we count aloud. Afterward I announce the results: Ten yeses and two noes.

Tom: "Karen, Kevin, don't you think the answer is rather obvious?"

I expect to wait through a long silence now. The key here is to shut my mouth. One of three things will happen: (1) Kevin and Karen will try to stall making the decision by asking for more time or asking a question to change the subject; (2) they will decide to go ahead; or, (3) they will give me an objection. Just as I expected, there is a silence in the room that seems to go on for some time while they think this over. Finally Kevin replies with a stall.

Kevin: "Tom, I'll tell you something. We're the kind of people who really need to think it over."

I hope you can see how this method, delivered with real warmth and sincerity, will be so valuable to your career. This is how all selling situations should be handled: In a relaxed, friendly, gentle and professional manner. Remember, it's not only what you say, but how you say it that creates a successful sales environment. However, sometimes even the warmest presentation, delivered with genuine care for the customer's needs can be met with "Well, we really need to think it over." How do you handle a situation where the prospect absolutely insists on "thinking it over"?

2. KEVIN "THINKS IT OVER"

Let's take the same prospects:

Tom: "That's fine, Kevin. Obviously, you wouldn't take the time to think it over; unless you were seriously interested, would you?"

Kevin: "Oh, we're interested. We just really need to think about this before we decide."

Tom: "Since you are interested, may I assume that you will give it very careful consideration?"

Karen: "Of course, we will."

Tom: "Kevin, you're not telling me this just to get rid of me, are you?"

Kevin: "No. I'm not trying to get rid of you. We like the house, but we have to think it over."

Tom: "Just to clarify my thinking, what is it about the house that you want to think over? Is it the value of the home? Is it the neighborhood, etc.?"

Ask about every benefit of the home. Every time they say no, they are that much closer to a yes, aren't they? Kevin and Karen answer no to every benefit, so what is it that they want to think over? In most cases, it will come down to money. Either the home will be too expensive, they won't be comfortable with the large initial investment or they may be worried about their credit and getting qualified for the loan.

Tom: "Well, could it be the financing or even the initial investment that you want to think over?"

Karen: "Yes. We might have another baby and I'm not sure if we should make a financial commitment like this right now."

3. REDUCTION TO THE RIDICULOUS

This consummation technique is used when you have isolated that it's a money objection that is preventing the final agreement. Let's stay with Karen and Kevin, in the real estate office:

Karen: "Tom, I just feel that this home costs too much."

Tom: "Today, most things seem to. Can you tell me about how much too much you feel it is?"

We salespeople tend to look at the total investment when presented with "It costs too much." This is trouble. Instead, go for the difference. If someone plans on spending $20,000 for a car and the car they are looking at is $22,000, the problem isn't $22,000, it's $2,000.

Karen: "We really wanted to spend around $110,000, and I don't feel we can go as high as $115,000."

Tom: "So, Karen and Kevin, what we are really talking about is $5,000, aren't we?"

Kevin: "$5,000. Right. That's exactly what I'm concerned about."

Hand them your calculator. This is a good way to get them involved as you work out the finances.

Tom: "Karen, do you think it would be safe to assume this would be your dream home and you could be happy here for a long time assuming everything else was right?"

Karen: "Probably. I think it would be a great place to raise the kids."

Tom: "Let's just say that you are going to live in this beautiful home for 20 years. Would you say that's about right?"

Kevin: "20 years. Yes, that would be about right."

Tom: "Let's divide that $5,000 by 20. Okay, we get $250, don't we?"

Kevin: "Yes."

Tom: "And would you say that you would actually be in the home 50 weeks per year, allowing for two weeks of vacation each year, of course."

Kevin: "Yeah. Right."

Tom: "That makes the difference in the investment $5.00 per week. So, now we have 7 days in each of those weeks and when we divide $5 by 7, what do we get?"

Karen:	"Seventy-one cents."
Tom:	"Kevin, do you and your family drink much soda?"
Kevin:	"Sure. You know how kids are. We probably go through at least one six-pack per day."
Tom:	"How much are sodas these days?"
Karen:	"Around $2.00 a six pack."
Tom:	"Karen, Kevin, wouldn't you agree that the benefits and the enjoyment you will get out of this wonderful home are worth 71 cents a day? Do you think we should let 71 cents stand in the way of all the family memories you will make there, for less than it costs your family to have three sodas per day?"
Kevin:	"When you look at it that way, I guess it doesn't seem to be such a significant amount."
Tom:	"Then we've agreed, haven't we? Now, let's get to work to get you out of your existing house and into this <u>beautiful home</u> by the <u>holidays</u> so you and your <u>family</u> can begin <u>building memories</u> right away. By the way, would the 10th, or the 12th, be the best closing date for both of you?"

Notice the words that are underlined? These are the key words that create pleasant pictures in the minds of these buyers. They may have said they wanted to be in the home by November 1st. That gives you the license to address the upcoming holidays which almost always creates warm feelings for the buyer.

This role play also demonstrates how easy it is to flow from one consummation to another. It's important that you know as many consummation stories as there are objections. Create your own consummation stories and tailor them to your product or service. The important thing is to be prepared.

4. SIMILAR SITUATION

What could be a better story than telling your prospects of another couple who had all the same concerns and indecision that they have, but those people decided to go ahead and now are so glad they did?

"John, Jennifer. I know you're hesitant about the financial commitment of buying a home when you have your first baby on the way.

You know, I had another family looking for the perfect home, just about a year ago. We searched and searched and they just couldn't decide on a home.

One day we looked at a beautiful home and they got very excited about it. I asked them if they felt this was the home for them and they agreed that it was a great house. I also asked if they wanted to begin the process of owning that great home. Bob thought we should go ahead, but Kathy was afraid that the home might be a bit larger than they really needed. She thought they could get by in a smaller home and she wasn't sure that she wanted to move before their baby came.

Well, they decided to go ahead and were amazed at how much space the baby things took up. Bob and Kathy were so glad that they had decided to invest in the bigger home when they did.

Now, you'd like to be all settled in your new home before your baby comes, wouldn't you?"

I hope you can see how important it is to develop and know multiple consummation stories. Let's continue from here:

5. STATE OF THE ECONOMY

The condition of the United States economy always gets a lot of attention. Whenever the stability of the economy is in question, you can count on mounting fear when it comes to ownership decisions by the general public. You will probably encounter decision-makers who are fearful of expenditures until they can foresee better times coming.

Salesperson: "Yes, I know there is a lot of concern about the
                          state of the economy. The very word "recession"
                          breeds fear of spending, which in turn, creates more
                          of a recession as everyone struggles to hang on to
                          their money, don't you agree?
                          Tell me, did you know that a great percentage of
                          today's giant corporations and very successful
                          business people began their success momentum

during times of economic hardship? While others were fearful and pessimistic of what was happening, these people had the courage and foresight to say yes.

What it basically comes down to is this, "N" and "O" are the first two letters of the word nothing. Nothing can be achieved by the word "No" and most people don't like what that word nothing implies. May I assume that you don't like the meaning of no either?"

Prospect: "Sure. But I'll tell you Tom, I just can't spend that kind of money until I start seeing some signs of recovery."

So again, you've isolated that the prospect is procrastinating due to a money objection. Now this is another situation where you can "Bridge" to the Reduction to the Ridiculous consummation story.

6. MONEY OR THINGS

To be used when they express concern about depreciation.

Salesperson: "Everything depreciates. Cars, homes, retirement plans, products. Everything. Even money itself depreciates, doesn't it? I wouldn't want you to make this decision if I weren't so sure from what you've told me that you would benefit from this for many years to come. Today, most of us must make the same decisions. Do we want to retain all of our spendable income and watch its value depreciate, or do we want to invest some of it for things that will provide enjoyment for our families and ourselves?"

7. COMPETITIVE EDGE

Salesperson: "Mr. Prospect, please realize that many of your competitors are facing the same challenges today that you are. Isn't it interesting when an entire industry is fighting the same forces, some companies do a better job of meeting those challenges than others? My entire objective here today has been to help provide you with a competitive edge. Gaining a competitive edge, no matter how large or small, makes good business sense, doesn't it?"

8. THE BEST THINGS IN LIFE

This approach is used when the prospects are procrastinating making the decision to get involved with the product or service.

> **Salesperson:** Isn't it true that the only time you have ever benefitted from anything in your life has been when you have said Yes instead of No? You said yes to your marriage (Optional: and I can see how happy you are.) You said yes to your job, your home, your car -- all the things that I'm sure you truly enjoy. You see, when you say yes to me, it's not really me you are saying yes to, but all the benefits that we offer, and those are the things you really want for your family, don't you agree?"

I will give you 14 more stories a little later in this chapter to study. These stories are not meant to talk anybody into anything they don't **want** or need. Their sole purpose is to help people make a decision that they want to make. Remember, they wouldn't invest their valuable time talking with you about your product or service if they didn't want it. Prospects are just like us. We all need help making decisions. Think about it. How many things have you been talked into owning that you really didn't want at all? Again, if you are like me, not very many. The truth is, very few people are ever talked into, or sold something they don't really want. If it's a major purchase, it's usually difficult to sell your prospects even if they do **want** it.

Most sales image problems arise from salespeople who push to involve people in things they don't want. Problems also arise when an unscrupulous salesperson lies about what the product is, what it will do, and through deceit takes advantage of the buyer's trust so they end up with something other than what they thought they were getting. The jails are full of these types of people. They let their search of the dollar get in the way of their service to the customer. If you put service to your customer ahead of money, you will always come out on top.

You may be wondering if I feel the use of these consummation questions, assumptive statements, and stories are in the best interest of my customer? In my experience, I would have to definitely say, "Yes." I have done a lot of selling, and I always took my customers' interests to heart. I knew they would get the truth from me, as well as, great service. I felt if I didn't help them make a decision to buy from me, I would have no control over what happened to them when they went elsewhere.

What I really want is to help every consumer have a positive image of the sales industry. I knew that positive image would be there if the customers were given the most professional service available, and I was the one to provide it. That's why I worked harder than many of my associates to consummate sales that I knew were in the best interest of my customers. This, obviously, would not include selling them anything they didn't want. However, if all things were right, I would do everything I could to help them get over the hills of fear and procrastination.

Now, let me ask you a question. Drawing on your own experience, have you had appreciation for sales professionals who helped you make a decision? Have you been happy enough to recommend those sales professionals to others? Of course you have! We all have. What I ask is that you set a goal to become someone people would not hesitate to recommend. Become someone customers seek out as an expert in your field.

Since the emphasis of this book is **quiet** power, I believe I must remind you to put yourself in second place. If you don't understand why you were unsuccessful with a prospect, look at your attitude, choice of words and style of delivery. Was it that of a lion or a lamb? Keep on reading because we will be talking about attitudes in a later chapter. Always remember: Put their needs before yours. That is the attitude of a professional. If you are not doing this already, please be aware that for things to change, you'll need to change.

The End is Really a Beginning

I'm going to tell you about this again and again. Consummating the sale starts at the beginning of the transaction, when you first make contact with the customers. If you are weak on original contact, qualifying, handling objections, presentations, or any other area of the sales process or are generally weak in asking pertinent questions, I don't care how great a salesperson you **think** you are, you are costing your prospect, yourself and your company a lot of money, loss of time and aggravation. The simple fact is, **no one** consummates every sale, but just think of how much better you can become when you put your best effort into it. A perfect ending needs a perfect beginning.

That is what consummation of the sale is all about and it doesn't need to be complicated either. Here are some examples of simple questions you can ask that will often lead to the consummation of the sale without the need for a story.

CONSUMMATION QUESTIONS

1. Basic Oral Question

Define the needs you can fill and ask a question. "You had said that you start your new job on the 21st. Would the 10th or the 12th be the best closing date for you?"

Another example is this: "John, Mary, I'm excited to help you take a major step toward financial independence. We can do that with your approval right here."

2. The Basic Written Consummation

This is an effective consummation if you use order forms. Walk in with a leather binder. Have an order form under a cardboard protector. This allows you to flip to it instantly when the time is right.

Prospect:	"Does it come in blonde wood?"
Champion:	"Is blonde the best color accent for your furniture?"
Prospect:	"Yes. I think that would look fantastic."
Champion:	"Let me make a note of that."

Now you write it down on the order form. Careful, some people might get panicky at seeing you filling out a form.

Prospect: "What are you doing? I haven't agreed to anything yet."

Champion: "Mrs. Palmer, I like to organize my thoughts to keep everything in order. I do that on the paper work so I don't forget anything." (If it suits your product or service add: "particularly anything that could cost you time or money.") Then continue.

Go into every consummation sequence by asking a reflex question. Remember, a reflex question is one they can answer without thinking. When you reach the point in the sales cycle where you can comfortably ask for specific information to write on your form, you should have earned the right to use their first name. If you're not sure if you've earned that right, you probably haven't. Never jump into the familiarity of using that first name unless you're certain it's OK with them.

Champion: "Mary, do you have a middle initial?"

Prospect: "It's K."

If you are dealing with a corporate executive, a good reflex question is to ask for the company's complete name and address. If the executive hands you their card and let's you copy all the information, congratulations, you are moving ahead.

You might be thinking that it would be better to make notes on the legal pad. If you write everything on a legal pad, eventually you will have to put it on an order form anyway.

Always use a legal pad and your paperwork. Let them stop you from writing. It doesn't hurt you. It helps you. It helps you because it shows the prospect that you are a professional salesperson, who knows how to get things done. Keep filling out that order form. By the time you've finished your presentation, the form will be close to completely filled out. In most cases, the forward momentum you've been developing while completing this form will be enough to get it approved. If they get used to seeing you writing on the order form, you're almost home. The problem many salespeople have is they don't start writing soon enough. By that I mean you should begin writing on your paperwork when you begin your qualification questions. If you feel better using a qualifying form that you custom make for your product or service, go ahead and do so. However, please be certain to explain to the customer the reason you are asking for this information is to help them make a better decision.

3. Sharp Angle

This carries the Porcupine technique, discussed earlier, to a higher level of effectiveness. Instead of merely answering a question with a question as with the standard Porcupine, answer with one that, if they reply the way their original question indicates they will, they've bought it.

Prospect: "If I decide I want this boat, can you handle delivery by Memorial Weekend?"

You: "If I can guarantee delivery by Memorial Weekend, I bet you can guarantee me that you will be prepared to have a great time enjoying the holiday on your new boat, can't you?"

In this example of Sharp-Angling, you're still leading your prospect, Mr. Stewart, toward buying a boat.

Mr. Stewart: "If I decided to go with this boat, I'd want delivery by May 15. Could you handle that?" (Now the average salesperson would be tempted to jump in, say yes, whether he could or not. Pay close attention to how a professional takes advantage of this same opportunity.)

Champion: "If I could guarantee delivery by May 15, are you prepared to approve the paperwork today?" Or if you really don't know if you can make delivery on that date you may want to respond by saying, "If I could guarantee delivery by May 15, and I am not certain yet that I can, are you prepared to approve the paperwork today?"

Then the Champion knows to remain silent until Mr. Stewart answers.

To use the Sharp-Angle method, you must first have them make a demand or express a desire that you can meet. There are many demands or needs that you can Sharp Angle besides delivery.

Sharp-Angling involves two pivotal points: (a) you must know what benefits you can deliver, and (b) it is critical to the Sharp-Angle that you know when that delivery can be made.

Sharp-Angle Danger

A dangerous part of the Sharp-Angle is that you may be tempted to apply it before enough qualification information has been gathered or rapport has been built. I don't recommend its use at that step in the selling process for obvious reasons. It could easily be a case of too much too soon. At that stage, some people might be offended because the method is not very smooth and can be interpreted as being overly aggressive. However, if the prospect's thinking and the rapport is right, it's a wonderful way to get agreement early in the sales process.

For example, if they say, "Can you get it for me in red?" and you reply, "Are you ready to go ahead today if I can?" They may say "yes", or they may say, "I might be, but I will need a lot more information."

Before you say, "Will you go ahead if I can", you must be absolutely sure that you can deliver your product. It won't do much good if you say you can deliver if you can't. One of the reasons why a Champion can outsell the average salesperson is because they know more about their products and what their company can deliver.

How do they get this information? The answer depends on your product, the company, and your attitude. Many salespeople tend to make enemies in the production department and on the shipping dock by promising clients things the company can't deliver. When the client gets angry over a missed delivery date, the production department or the shipping dock usually takes the blame. Know what your company can deliver. Thank the people in your company who help you get your job done especially if it calls for extra effort on their part in order for you to make the sale.

4. Higher Authority

Every happy client is a potential higher authority for another prospect. This consummation method is very effective if you know it thoroughly and set it up correctly. No matter what your product or service, all you need do is to adapt the wording to your own style of selling.

The higher authority must be exactly that-- someone who is respected by and known to the prospect. The prospect doesn't have to know the higher authority personally, but they must know of their existence and position. If you sell industrial equipment, you'll want a prominent decision-maker at a well-known company; if you sell advertising, you'll want a high-profile business person.

Here are the steps for using this close successfully:

(a) **Select your higher authority figure**.

You should constantly be on the lookout for higher authority figures. Let's work on an example, you're the sales-record-smasher for Builtgreat Computer Systems.

A prominent businessman in the area invested in a computer system for his company, Marketshare, Inc. and is very pleased with the system's performance and increased productivity. This businessman, George Steele, is an ideal higher authority figure for anyone interested in your computers.

(b) **Recruit your higher authority figure**.

On one of your visits to Marketshare, Inc., after they have had plenty of time to know the system inside and out, you ask George Steele if he'd be willing to share his knowledge of your product with other business people. George agrees because you've done a solid sales and service job for him on a good product, and you've assured him that you'll only call when you need help with an occasional prospect who may be in a similar situation. In other words, you promise not to bother him if you're working on selling a two-computer system to a small business.

(c) **Line up your higher authority figure for the specific sales situation**.

You're out to update the computer system at Southwest Advertising with your newest system. Mary Phillips is the decision-maker there. While planning your appointment with Mary, you decide that you might need the higher authority figure confirmation, so you call George Steele to determine if he'll be available to take a phone call while you're with Mary Phillips. With George's cooperation, you complete your plans for a powerful presentation to Mary at Southwest.

(d) **Effective use of the higher authority figure confirmation**.

You know that Mary will have similar concerns about your system that George Steele had.

Will the software that makes your systems superior be the right one to increase productivity for Southwest?

Is your service department as good as you say it is?

In planning your presentation you know that Mary will have specific technical questions.

The primary purpose of your interview with Mary Phillips is to isolate the specific technical and other reservations she has about your equipment and company. Once you have clarified these questions in her mind and you have agreed that these are all reasons that cause her to question the idea of installing your system now, you're ready to bring in a higher authority. It's vital to make that list of reasons specific, and to get agreement that they are all the reservations Mary has. Write them out on a piece of paper.

Salesperson: "Do you know George Steele of MarketShare, Inc.?"

Prospect: "No, but I know of the company."

Salesperson: "George is the owner, and he is a client of mine. Mary, so that I can relieve your mind of some of the questions you may have about the system or our services, would you be offended if we called George and asked him those questions. You see, he had the same concerns you did before he invested in our system?"

When George is on the phone, tell him, "I'm here at Southwest Advertising with Mary Phillips and she has some questions about Builtgreat." Then hand the phone to Mary and let her take it from there. She has the list of questions in front of her so nothing will be missed.

(e) **Close after the call**.

Once George Steele has discussed the technicalities and reassured Mary that the Builtgreat computers are performing well in his office, Mary's objections aren't there anymore. When the phone call ends, you're in a position to ask, "By the way, what delivery date is most convenient, the first or the tenth?"

If something happens and George Steele isn't available even though you set it up with him, after all his job still comes first, you may not be able to consummate the sale today. Try to set up a specific recontact time, when you are present with Mary, or arrange a conference call.

Take a copy of Mary's objections and "hot buttons" with you so you'll be able to get back to where you left off at the start of the recontact. Remember to do a brief recap with Mary before getting George on the line.

Some salespeople turn away from the higher authority confirmation because they feel that all competitors hate each other and won't cooperate. There are exceptions, but as a rule, most people at competing companies are friendly. They respect each other and there is always the possibility that they may be looking for another job in their industry some day and could use the connection. If you do happen to run into a case of bad blood between competitors, simply back off.

Don't settle for just one higher authority because you can wear out any one person with overuse. When you do your job with the utmost professionalism, you'll find that most clients will be happy to help you out, it's an ego boost for them to be considered a higher authority.

CALCULATE FIGURES WITH FINESSE

Champions always do their selling math with a calculator. No matter how confident you are in your mathematical abilities, always use a calculator. Know your formulas and figures so that you can quickly provide any numerical information that your prospect might be requesting. A prospect, seeing you punching numbers into your calculator, probably won't question the figures. But, if you start furiously scratching numbers on paper with a pencil, the prospect will be growing uncomfortable sitting and watching you do this. Even worse, if you just rattle off figures out of your head, they may doubt you. They will be looking over your shoulder to double-check your math.

CONFIRMATION QUESTIONS

Confirmation questions are just special questions. When answered, they will tell you that the prospect has reached a high level of interest and that they are willing to go further. When you ask a confirmation question, you're looking for answers to give you positive stimulus. Here are three confirmations:

1. The Alternate Advance

"Ms. Hall, which delivery date would be best for you, the eighth or the 13th?" When she says, "I'd need to have it in my warehouse by the tenth", what's happened? As long as you can meet that delivery date, she owns it. Stay on course in your consummation sequence and you're all set. If she's uncertain, she'll raise an objection here or try to change the subject.

Another example is this: "Jim, would you be the one trained on the use of the new system, or would you want someone else to be involved?" When he tells you who to train, he's going ahead.

2. Erroneous Conclusion

A Champion listens throughout the presentation for anything said that he can use later for an erroneous conclusion test close. As we explained earlier, in a test consummation, all you're going for is to test their buying temperature -- to see if it's warm enough to go ahead. For example, you're in a home selling home improvements. During your demonstration the wife tells her husband, "Honey, my mother is coming in July. If we decide what we want today, we ought to have it finished by then."

Many salespeople would ignore that remark, or regard it as an interruption. But the professional hears it, and remembers it. Later, the salesperson might smile at the wife and say:

Salesperson:	"I can see that you're kind of excited about this addition. Now, your mother is coming in August, is she?"
Prospect:	"No, in July."
Salesperson:	"So the first week in June would be the best time to get started?"

Prospect:	"Yes."
Salesperson:	"Let me make a note of that."

You can use the erroneous conclusion test close on size, color, windows, almost anything. The wife might have said:

Prospect:	"I think I'd like a bay window on the south wall."

Later, you can use that and say:

Salesperson:	"Let's see. You said you wanted the bay window on the east wall..."
Prospect:	"No! I want it on the south wall."
Salesperson:	"Yes, that's right. Let me make a note of that." Put that information on your paperwork too. If you make a mistake and they correct you, they may be agreeing to move forward by letting you write down the correction.

Let me make a note here. The purpose of this method is not to tell a lie or trick the customer. I would never teach that. It's simply a test for you to determine if the prospect is sincere in moving ahead. They wouldn't correct you if they weren't. If you are uncomfortable at all in using this method, don't.

3. The Porcupine

We discussed this earlier in the "Questioning" chapter. Aside from being a good information gatherer, it's a terrific confirmation question. Let's look at a car dealership example:

A young woman is walking through your car lot looking at convertibles. Suddenly she stops, points at a car, and says:

Prospect:	"This is the convertible I'm interested in. Do you have it in red?"

This situation occurs quite often.

Salesperson:	(This is how the average salesperson would answer.) "If we don't have it in red, I can call around and get one for you in a hurry."

When a salesperson gives an answer like that, are they looking to help themselves, or the customer? The professional salesperson answers:

Salesperson:	"Linda, would you like it in Red-Hot Red or Cranberry Red?" Or, "Red is one of the most

popular colors in this model. If I can locate one for you in red, would you be ready to go ahead with the purchase now?"

What's she going to say? She has already told you that she's interested in the convertible and she wants it in red. She'll most likely give you a positive answer so you will be moving ahead.

As a general rule, after each question and answer you should be moving closer to the consummation. If you are not, your questions may be off base or you may not be listening to the customer's answers carefully enough.

As I have said before, it is extremely valuable to record yourself and find out if your questions are pertinent and you are taking advantage of all the information the customer is giving you.

Keeping in mind that the focus of this book is quiet power, take a look at this next example. This is what an ineffective salesperson considers consummation.

Prospect: "Do you have this in navy blue?"

Sales Rookie: "If I can get it for you in navy blue, will you buy it?"

Prospect: "No. I'm not buying anything right now. Leave your materials and I'll call you if I'm interested. Thanks for coming."

The sales rookie approached this consummation with all the finesse of a bowling ball approaching the pins. **"If I can get it for you in navy blue, will you buy it?"** is a say-no question that will reverse your positive, forward direction. Closing techniques like this will instantly create pressure for the prospect. This technique is commonly known as the Sharp Angle close and as we've already discussed, it can be dangerous if not handled with finesse.

Do you remember what we said about pressure? Too much pressure and you've lost the sale. A sales professional would handle the same situation with gentle strength:

Prospect: "Do you have this in navy blue?"

Salesmaster: "Is that the color you would require?"

Prospect: "Yes. It is."

Salesmaster: "Let me make a note of that." (As he writes the
                        information on the order form.)

CONSUMMATE WITH EMPATHY

The definition of empathy is: Understanding intimately the feelings,
thoughts, and motives of another.

Empathy is so important in professional selling. Empathy is putting
yourself into the prospect's shoes. It's knowing and feeling what your
prospect is feeling. It's knowing exactly how to proceed depending on the
information the individual prospect has given you.

Until you develop empathy for your customers, until you develop the
skill of calling for and getting a favorable agreement that we call consummation, you will probably not make it in selling. The customer should
feel you understand and care about helping them solve their problems, not
that you are just looking for a sale.

As a professional salesperson you must truly believe that you can satisfy the prospect's needs. You must see the benefits, features, and limitations of your product or service from your prospect's view; you must
weigh things on the prospect's scale of values, not your own; you must
realize what is important to the prospect.   As we discussed earlier, they
must always be the stars of the show.

After you have qualified them and discovered what they want, you
must attend to your own need--the need to radiate confidence that you
know exactly how to help them.

WHEN SHOULD YOU CONSUMMATE THE SALE?

There's a certain electricity in the air when the prospect is ready to
invest, but here are some other things to watch for:
*   The prospects have been moving along at a certain pace and
     suddenly they slow the pace way down. (They're slowing down
     to think it over.)

* Or, they start speeding up. (They're excited to move ahead.)
* Suddenly they start asking lots of questions. (They will only ask questions about things they are interested in.)
* Positive stimulus. Some people immediately start asking questions about initial investment, delivery, etc. before they settle on one particular model. They feel safe doing this, because they know you can't sell them everything. If they ask these questions after you know exactly what they want, it's positive stimulus.

Go for a test consummation after getting positive stimulus. If you feel that your customers are ready to consummate the sale, try a test question to make sure you are reading the stimulus correctly. As you get more experience in selling, you will become more proficient at reading body language and other buying signals. This can be good and bad.

Some people start relying too much on looking for a positive reading, that they try to short-cut the other steps such as qualifying or demonstration. <u>When you do this, it is very difficult to go back and attempt to do these steps later.</u> You will invariably lose many sales. While it is important to become better at knowing when to consummate the sale, each prospect should be given your full presentation to assure you don't come up short at the end. Then move ahead with the consummation.

THE EIGHT MOST IMPORTANT WORDS IN THE ART OF CONSUMMATION

Whenever you ask a consummation question, shut up!

When you ask a question from which you expect an answer to confirm that the prospects are going ahead with the purchase, you want one of two things to happen:

1. The prospect gives you a "yes", or an answer that would confirm they are going ahead with the sale.

OR

2. They will give you an objection or ask for more information to enable them to make a decision.

If you start talking before they've answered, you lose control of the negotiations. And, you have gained nothing. You don't have a confirmation to go ahead, or an objection, so your attempt to consummate the sale has been totally wasted.

Would you like delivery on the 15th or the 30th? They pause to think when would be the best time to have the product delivered. You get uncomfortable with the silence and you think, "They must be thinking they don't want it." So you panic and start saying, "Okay, how about if I give you another 5% off?" When the total investment wasn't what the prospect was considering in the first place. That's why you always wait for them to respond before you speak, after asking your consummation question. I hope you can see how important it is to keep quiet when you have asked your final consummation question.

If you start looking around or fidgeting, you'll be distracting the customer and letting them know how uncomfortable you are. Neither of these scenarios helps you move toward a successful consummation. Try to focus your stress in a way they will not see or recognize as a nervous action. For example, recite the abc's backwards to yourself, or maybe wiggle your toes--they can't see that. It can be that simple. I had a real problem with this, and I didn't even know what I was doing wrong, until Doug Edwards shouted the words SHUT UP at the audience.

The first time I tried it, I was prepared for the prospect's reaction. I expected them to sit there quietly. What I wasn't prepared for was the intensity of my own feelings. The silence that followed my final consummation question felt like being buried under a mountain, one stone at a time. Doug Edwards warned us that this is very uncomfortable until you get used to it, but I was surprised at how it affected me. I sat there with my insides churning. I was biting the inside of my lip, suddenly conscious of every nerve ending in my body. Finally, the prospect looked me straight in the eye and said yes. After that first time, I never again had much trouble sitting through the silence after asking my consummation question.

Here's how it goes. You're working with Carrie Walker, the purchasing agent for a medium-size manufacturer, and you feel she's ready for the consummation.

You: "Ms. Walker, now that we've covered everything, which would be more convenient, delivery by rail or truck?"

Now average salespeople can't wait more than 10-12 seconds before they buckle under and say something like:

"Well, okay, we can talk about that later." and continues talking.

Can you see how this can destroy the consummation situation?

Ms. Walker probably won't be sold now because she knows how to side-step the consummation question. She sits quietly for a few seconds and the salesperson cracks.

If you are made up of true Champion material, you can sit there all afternoon if you have to. Trust me, you'll rarely have to hang on more than 30 seconds. This is something you need to practice. It takes concentration to sit still and be silent, but **this is the most vital skill there is in selling**, and despite the fact that this is so easy to practice, few people do it. Practice right now so you are aware of how long is long. Then, when there is big money riding on your ability to remain quiet, you can sit there calmly. The most important things I can tell you about successfully consummating a sale would be to learn thoroughly all of the seven steps to selling. The end of the sales process really is a beginning of a successful relationship and the greatest "close" in the world isn't going to make up for errors in other areas.

FOURTEEN MORE CONSUMMATION STORIES FOR THE SALES PROFESSIONAL

1. "I can get it cheaper somewhere else."
Salesperson: "That may well be true, Mr. Kelly. In today's economy, we are all looking for the most value for our money, aren't we? One thing I have learned over the years is that the cheapest price is not always the

best value. Most people look for three things when making an investment:

1. The finest quality.
2. The best service.
3. The lowest price.

Mr. Kelly, I have yet to find a company that could honestly provide
the finest quality and the best service for the lowest price. I'm curious,
Mr. Kelly, would you mind if I asked which of these three benefits you'd
be willing to give up?"

2. Change is good.
Salesperson: "Tom, recently there has been talk of everyone having
to make too many choices.

Wouldn't you agree that making choices brings about change and that
change brings about fear?   When you think about it, isn't change our
greatest opportunity?

The choice of (name your product or service) will greatly increase
(name the benefits), don't you agree?

The bottom line though, is your ability to make the choice today and
immediately begin enjoying the benefits of change and growth opportunity immediately. Would you like delivery on the 10th or the 11th?"

3. The choice is yours.
Salesperson: "Mrs. Edwards, I can certainly understand what you are
feeling. With all the choices each of us face today, we worry about making a wrong decision. Sometimes, indecision can cost us more in time
and energy, than the wrong decision, can't it? In today's competitive environment, successful companies are facing the same challenges as any of
the lesser ones. The difference is, successful companies are successful
because they do a more effective job of meeting those business challenges.

My company can offer you (briefly name your top three benefits) and
help you to overcome many of your business challenges. With your

approval on this agreement, you'll be on your way to becoming a progressive company that meets challenges, pushes them aside, and moves ahead."

4. Take the lead.

Salesperson: "Mr. Peters, a former football coach in Philadelphia always had a sign above his desk that read, 'If you're not the lead dog, the scenery never changes.' Funny and true, don't you think?

You want your company to have the competitive edge, don't you? I can understand your hesitation, but from what you have told me, this (name your product or service) is exactly what your company needs to take the lead from your competitors."

5. You deserve the best.

Salesperson: "You know, Mrs. Chase, one thing that I've learned in serving the people of this community, is that the ones who tried to save a few dollars by investing in lesser-quality products usually ended up dissatisfied with the product. This dissatisfaction lingers long after the original investment is forgotten.

Isn't it worth a few extra dollars for a quality product and the best value available?"

6. Good is not enough.

Salesperson: "Mr. and Mrs. Prospect, as we discussed you had a concern with (whatever the area of concern).

Based on what you have told me, I would have to say that what you have now is good. When we compared the facts, we agreed that what you saw today was better, didn't we?

I have heard a saying that goes, 'If better is possible, good is not enough.' When it comes to ourselves and our families, good is not enough, is it?"

7. Maximum exposure.

Salesperson: "In times like this, money doesn't stop flowing, it merely changes direction. Every business is competing for the same dollars being spent. With all this competition, our research has shown that the company who can put and keep it's name in the mind of the public is the one that will succeed. Nowadays, exposure isn't a choice, it's a necessity. Effective exposure brings your company to mind first when the customer is ready to invest. Exposure brings your company a degree of familiarity to which the customer is drawn.

Understanding this, Mrs. Buyer, would you like your billboards on a 30- or 60-day rotation?"

8. "Maybe next year."

Salesperson: "Mr. Prospect, I understand that you'd rather wait until next year to invest. But have you ever heard the business philosophy that says, "There's only one reason to advertise this year - next year." I don't need to tell you how true this is. The business you gain now will move you towards even more success next year. Business momentum is what every company strives for, isn't it? Because you need to begin that success momentum this year, can you really afford to wait any longer?"

9. What's really important?

Salesperson: "Tom, with most households depending on two incomes these days, we've all had to make sacrifices. Most parents don't have a lot of time to spend with their children, not to mention their spouses. Sometimes we are so busy making a living, that we forget to make a life.

For such a small monthly investment, think of all the hours of happiness and enjoyment your family will have in your own backyard pool.

Tom, I am offering you an opportunity to create memories you and your family will cherish forever. Family is important to all of us, isn't it?"

10. "You have nothing to fear."

Salesperson: "Mr. and Mrs. Prospect, I'm sure you are aware that many savings and loans, credit unions and brokerage firms have gone under in the past few years. I understand that you are fearful of how your investments will be protected and that the income you set aside now will be available to you when you want it. Our company has the strongest financial rating in all categories by every service that rates financial institutions. This strength is your guarantee that your investment is safe, growing and will be here when you need it and that's what you are looking for, isn't it?"

11. "I don't want to switch."

Salesperson: "Mr. Buyer, I can appreciate your concern. Wouldn't you agree that most of us are afraid of the unknown? We all tend to become comfortable with what we have now and we are fearful of making changes.

Mr. Buyer, can you understand that if everyone thought this way, where would the world be? What if our forefathers never fought to get out from under British rule? I remember my father helping me to decide on which college to attend. I was terrified about leaving home and my family. I wanted everything to stay the same. Then my father said to me, Son, I know you're afraid but you can't get to second base by keeping a foot on first. He's right, isn't he? Many times, the first step to growth is change and growth is what you want for your business, isn't it?"

12. The Purchase Order Request

This is used primarily for industrial, commercial, and governmental sales. Once you have defined the needs you can fill, ask this question:

"By the way, what purchase order number will be assigned to this requisition?"

If they tell you they don't know, smile warmly and say, "What's the process for finding out?" In most industrial, commercial or governmental sales, you haven't made the sale until you get the P.O. number. So start hunting for it as soon as possible.

13. The Secondary Question

When used at the right moment, with the right people, this consummation can nail down the sale. Here's how to do it: Pose the major decision with a question, and without pausing, add another question that is an Alternate Advance/Involvement question that can only be answered if they are thinking in terms of after they own it.

"Can we agree, Dan, the only decision we have to make today is how soon you'll start enjoying these wonderful golf clubs? By the way, will you be playing public courses or do you belong to a private club?"

Let's try this technique on a service you're selling:

"As I see it, Dan, the only decision we have to make today is how soon you'll start enjoying the increased productivity of your employees when they start using our health club. By the way, will your employees be going to the club on Main Street, or the one on   Paradise Drive?"

You can easily adapt this format to any product or service. The major decision is introduced with these words:

"As I see it, the only decision we have to make today is how soon..." or "Can we agree, the only decision we have to make today is how soon..."

The major decision is then followed, without pause, by the Secondary Question that you introduce by saying, "By the way..." To use the Secondary Question successfully, you must:

(a) **State the major decision in terms of a benefit to the client.**

"The only decision...is how soon you'll start enjoying (the benefit)." Never pose the major decision in negative terms: "...how soon you'll stop throwing away money by..." Or, even worse, a thinly disguised attempt at humor: "...how soon you'll get on the ball and start saving money by ordering from me."

(b) **Avoid any pause between posing the major decision and ask-
     ing the Secondary Question.**

(c) **State the Secondary Question in terms of an Alternate
     Advance Involvement Question.**

Let's go over that. An Alternate Advance is any question that indicates a choice of answers, all of which confirm that they're going ahead. An Involvement Question is one that requires the prospect to make an ownership decision. Use one sentence that is both an Alternate Advance and an Involvement Question.

(d) **Prepare your consummation in advance.**

It will require some effort to create a Secondary Question for your offering that packs as much selling power. I doubt that there is any other sales activity that can make you more money in less time than developing an effective Secondary Question. When you have worked out your consummation, memorize the words until you can repeat them effortlessly. Don't try to wing it, a winner is always prepared.

   (e) **Use the casual format given here.**

The introductory phrases not only keep this consummation organized in your mind, they also help you to deliver the consummation properly. Your delivery when consummating a sale is so important, which brings us to:

   (f) **Deliver the consummation in a relaxed and alert manner.**

Practice the consummation until you can say it clearly and casually. The casual approach is the cornerstone of sales success. By casual, I do not mean careless. You must cultivate an alert but relaxed attitude that makes people feel comfortable.

In sales, you must ask questions in a non-threatening way. Make the prospect feel comfortable about giving you the information that you need. Remember, act like a lamb, sell like a lion.

If I could give you one consummation method that would work every time, this book would be worth millions of dollars, but no two selling situations are exactly the same. As I have told you again and again, a great consummation won't overcome a poor opening. Every step of the sale is vitally important because the sale, consummation process, or close, is just the final step of a sequence of events. All it is is a call for action.

Unfortunately, there isn't one consummation that will work every time. Even if there was one that worked 25% of the time, so many people would jump on it, the overuse would kill it within a very short time. So, it's essential that you learn multiple consummations.

Let's say that I just used the Ben Franklin balance sheet consummation and the prospect says, "I'll think it over." If I can't handle this, I'm in trouble. You must be able to know multiple consummations well enough to gently move from one to another.

14. The "It Isn't In The Budget"

Here's one that should be in every professional salesperson's collection. It's especially useful if you call on institutions or government agencies. It's designed to be used when you're working with the president, owner, or high-ranking executive.

You've gone through your presentation, everything has been going great and boom...they tell you they don't have the budget for it. Here's how you respond:

"Of course not. That's why I contacted you in the first place." Don't pause here. Now how you proceed depends on whether you are working with a private company, a non-profit institution, or a government agency. We'll look at the commercial and industrial use first.

Continuation for Use with Companies

"I'm sure that every well-managed company controls its costs with a carefully planned budget. Am I also right in assuming that the chief executive of such a productive, trend-setting company such as yours uses that budget as a guideline, not as a restraint?

You, as the chief executive, retain the right to flex that budget in the interest of your company, isn't that right?

What we have been discussing is a system that will give (name the prospect's company) an immediate and continuing competitive edge. Tell me, Mr. Ford, under these conditions will your budget flex, or is it a restraint?"

Continuation for Non-Profit Institutions and Government Agencies

"I'm aware that every well-managed institution controls its costs with a carefully planned budget. I'm also aware that your office (agency etc.) is responsive to the public's ever-changing needs. It's true, isn't it, that you have this reputation?"

When they respond, move on with, "This means that you, as the director of such an effective organization, must be using the budget more as a guideline rather than a restraint. How else could the public be gaining the benefits you are producing through your facility now?

I assume that, as the director, you have the right to flex the budget to allow your organization to carry out its responsibilities in the most efficient manner possible.

We have been discussing a system that will give (whatever your benefits are...). Tell me, Mr. Gates, under these conditions, will your budget flex, or is it a restraint?"

Get Comfortable with No

You must learn to understand and be comfortable with this to reach the Champion level in selling. A Champion knows that the "Say no first" reflex of all buyers is their source of security. The "no" that buyers flip out so easily is the raw material you will polish and refine into your success.

So, now you know. You know that you'll hear the word no every day of your career. You also know the enormous potential behind every no. Throw yourself into learning how to convert those negatives into positives. That's what this book and your success is all about--turning no into yes. The highest paid professionals never stop practicing, improving, and adding to their selling skills. Nothing will do more to improve your sales performance than having a collection of effective sales tools that you've practiced until you can deliver them without thinking.

Become a Full-Time Student of Selling

Watch the people around you. I can create a new consummation by watching parents interact with their children. Even better, watch how children lead their parents to a decision. Pay attention to your co-workers, people on TV, and people in airports. The possibilities are only limited by your imagination.

I can't tell you how much the concepts and techniques presented in this book can enrich your life. Reread it often with this idea in mind and you'll find new insights each time you do. Be willing to pay the price, and you will reach your goals.

Let's review what we have covered. To sum it up, <u>selling is what you say and how you say it</u>. Even the greatest words and questions are lost if delivered with the wrong tone of voice or bad body language.

You, as a salesperson, need to know how you sound and look to your customers, even if you have to ask. That's right. If a customer doesn't buy, ask for their advice on how you can improve. If you are lucky, someone may be honest and hurt your feelings, but help your income.

As you get better at questions and the concept of calm enthusiasm, you will begin to exude an unassuming confidence that portrays a modest, but dynamic quality that people want to be around. You are a salesperson, a professional problem-solver, just looking for problems to solve for your customers. Does this sound like the type of person you would like to buy from or know? Most of the great salespeople I have had the pleasure to train and know have this air of quiet confidence about them that inspires others to act.

You may wonder why we would include so many different ideas in one book or where they came from. Remember at the beginning of this chapter when we talked about consummations being nothing more than stories? Well, there are millions of stories and there are thousands of different selling situations, so why shouldn't there be as many ways to consummate the sale?

If you were to attend one of our advanced three-day Academies, you would sit with and learn with many of the top salespeople in the country (earning six-figure incomes). Before those three days were over you would not only understand consummating the sale much better, but you would be writing your own consummation stories. Many of these students say this course increased their understanding of selling tenfold. I think after going this far in this book you'd agree selling is a learned skill quite unlike having a pleasing personality or the gift of gab.

CHAPTER 8
SELF MANAGEMENT

Time is Our Most Valuable Resource

Take a look at that last statement. Do you believe it? Unfortunately, many people have not come to this realization yet, and until they do they will continue to fritter their days and nights away and then wonder where all the time has gone. If you doubt the importance the subject of time plays in our world, just take a look around you.

Have you walked through the grocery store lately? The package labels that used to read "New and Improved" now say "Instant" or "Microwaveable". In fact, when you look at cooking directions on frozen foods, the microwave instructions now come before those for the conventional oven. The frozen food aisle used to be a small freezer case in the back of the store with just a few frozen vegetables or juice. In most stores, it now consumes nearly a third of their floor space, and is usually placed in the middle of the store for shoppers' convenience. All for the sake of saving time.

Mail order, TV and computerized shopping have recently taken a large chunk of the retail market. Why? Because it's much easier for busy people to thumb through a catalog or make a few phone calls than to trek from store to store sorting through hundreds of racks for what they want.

Everyone is searching for more time. The value of time has increased dramatically in recent years. It's the old adage of supply and demand. The busier we all become, the more time we need. If you ask any sales professional to name one thing that would make their lives easier, the overwhelming response would be **more time**. If you had more time to do the things you **need** to do, there's a good chance you would generate more income to do the things you want to do. Or would you?

Are you the type of person who would simply waste more time if you had it? Have you ever noticed the less time you have, the more you seem to get done? Average salespeople often spend their time foolishly doing unproductive, busy work--then wonder where their day went and why they got very little accomplished. The key word is they **spent** their time instead of **investing** it. Let's look at the difference.

Spending Time vs. Investing Time

There's a big difference in connotation between these two words, isn't there? What do you think of when you **spend** money? Usually you think of the loss of money rather than the benefits that you will enjoy from whatever it was you spent your money on. Now look at the word **invest**. That term signifies a return, doesn't it? You don't focus on the loss of money, but rather the gain of the product or service you will receive. Doesn't it stand to reason, if you are spending your time rather than investing it, you will focus on the lost time, rather than the personal gain? It all goes back to how you value time.

If you have never put a dollar value on time before, maybe this will open your eyes to a few truths. Let's see what your time is really worth. To determine your hourly rate, follow this simple equation: <u>Gross Income</u> divided by <u>Total Annual Working Hours</u> = <u>Hourly Rate</u>.

For example, if your annual income is $30,000, the value of each hour in your work week would be worth $14.42. If you spend just one hour each day of a work week on unproductive activity, you will have spent approximately $3605 a year on nothing. And, that is exactly what you will have to show for it--nothing. Can you afford to waste 12% of your annual income because you choose not to manage your time? This amount doesn't even take into consideration all the future business you lost because you spent time rather than investing it.

Now that we have established a correlation between how you spend your time and how much money you make, why don't we discover the advantages to investing your time wisely. As salespeople, we know that we often don't see immediate financial pay-off from our time invested. For example, when I was selling real estate, I invested my time prospecting, demonstrating property, and getting agreements approved, but I saw no return until the final transaction was completed and my broker had the check. This could be weeks and in some cases, months later.

During the period between my invested time and my financial reward, I sometimes lost sight of my goals. The longer the period between sales and pay-off, the more difficult it is to stay focused on investing our time wisely.

It's a normal occurrence in sales that when salespeople invest time in their customers, they begin to think of their returns. It is hard to keep your mind on a continued quest of more time invested, if you don't foresee those returns. The important thing is to recognize this trait in yourself and learn how the top professionals handle it. Professionals find a way to reward themselves for their time invested along the way.

Time Management or Self Management?

Management of time is really management of self, isn't it? If you are shaking your head no, stop and think about this for a moment. When did you last control time? Can you stop time, or even slow it down? No way. Can you negotiate with time? If you have figured this out, you should be writing a book instead of reading one. Time is relentless. It is a non-respecter of persons. Professional salespeople have no more time to invest than anyone else, and they are successful without controlling time. So, if you can't control time, what is all this about? Well, you can't control time, but you can control how **you** invest your time.

For example, many salespeople spend time traveling. You may be asking, "If this is a requirement on my job, how can I avoid it?" Well, you may have no control over the time you spend on the road, but you can choose to use that time to listen to motivational tapes, or educational tapes; thereby, you have managed to turn your expenditures into investments. You have invested your time to further your professional education. By doing this, you have created opportunities to increase your income by practicing new selling techniques. Now, that's an investment.

Another way to manage yourself when you find you must spend time traveling is to cluster your appointments. By organizing your presentations, or customer service appointments by location, you can save a lot of travel. If your travel time is primarily inner-city, you may want to schedule it so you are not stuck in rush-hour traffic. Taking side streets and back roads may lead you to previously unfound business opportunities. I'm sure if you invest time, planning your time, you will think of dozens of ways to manage yourself more efficiently.

If you believe those professional salespeople who practice time management are fanatical workaholics who leave no time for personal relaxation, you are mistaken. In actuality, it is just the opposite. Professionals who practice sound time management operate more efficiently, thereby, creating more time for personal endeavors.

Make Time to Plan Time

Another common complaint from salespeople who do not practice effective time-management is that they do not have time to plan their time. You often hear, "How can I take that time out of my busy day to plan, when I never have a spare moment?"

If you don't make time for planning and self-improvement, you might as well plan to earn the same income you earn today for the rest of your life. Is that what you really want? I don't think so.

It is a proven fact that by taking the time to plan, you will save 20-30 times the time expended in the planning process. Let me illustrate to you what I mean. A study was done on how managers planned their time. They found that managers who invested only 5 minutes planning a specific task, would spend 55 minutes to complete it. Those managers who invested 15 minutes on the planning process, spent only 30 minutes completing it. Look at the time saved--15 minutes. I would say that the time invested planning was well worth it, wouldn't you?

Sometimes the problem is that you don't know what to invest time in and what not to. If you have your personal, family and career goals mapped out, those goals will help you determine exactly the most beneficial way to invest your time.

In case you don't already have that done, I'll cover some basic goal setting ideas in Chapter 10. For now, let's categorize the things we choose spend time on into three areas: (1) immediate, (2) secondary, and (3) relatively unimportant. Even though these are the three main categories, let's not forget emergency situations. Although emergencies are rare, it's wise to build some flexibility into our schedules to allow for them.

Immediate Activities

These are only, and I do stress only, those things that you must complete today. If you clutter your mind with things that should be secondary activities it's possible some of your immediate activities will be neglected or not given the full attention they require. How do you know which things are immediate activities, and which ones can be put aside? Ask yourself these questions to help you determine your immediate activities:

1. If I could achieve only three or four of these activities today, which ones would they be?
2. Which activities will yield the highest pay-off or rewards?
3. Which of these activities would complicate my tomorrow if they were not achieved today?
4. Which of these activities could be delegated to someone else, thereby, leaving me more time to generate more business or enhance my personal relationships? For example: If yard work is not your hobby or a form of relaxation for you, pay someone else to do it for you while you do something more productive with that time.
5. Which activities, if postponed, would damage my relationship with customers or business associates?

You should have your immediate activities in front of you at all times. If you can't see what needs to be accomplished today because you have buried yourself under other less important work, it could get lost in the shuffle, and so could your business.

The following example is a simple form that will allow you to keep your immediate daily plans in focus. Make sure you use something along this order in your daily planner and most importantly **look at it every day**.

DAILY TIME AUDIT

															TOTAL HOURS
Prospecting															
Presenting															
Paperwork															
Planning															
Meetings															
Telephone															
Face to Face															
Servicing															
Travelling															
Letters															
Thank You's															
Interruptions															
Lunch															
Personal															
Other															

Notes: _____

_____

_____

_____

_____

_____

_____

_____

_____

Secondary Activities

It is usually a little easier to determine this group of activities. Some may be closer to immediate than others, so put those at the top of this pile or activity list. Again, you are using a simple method of prioritizing. It's important that you place secondary papers or other items in their designated location. By that I mean not on the top of your desk where they can distract you. Don't allow yourself to become preoccupied with piles of paperwork. This will only cause you stress and confuse you as to what needs immediate attention.

Relatively Unimportant Activities

You will be surprised how hard this pile of paperwork or list of activities is to determine. We tend to think everything needs our attention, or it wouldn't come our way. This is simply not true. There are many unimportant activities that others pass to you to take care of, or ones that will have a way of working themselves out if given a little time. By putting them in your relatively unimportant category, you may never have to **spend** time on these things when you should be **investing** time on your immediate activities.

For example, how many times has an associate come to you with a problem wanting your assistance, only to find out they didn't want your assistance? They wanted you to take the problem on as yours. What begins as a favor then ends up as a real chore. Their worries become your worries. While I am not suggesting you never help an associate, I will caution you about taking on the work that should be their responsibility. If you help an associate, make sure that you are compensated, either financially or by an exchange of help on one of your projects. Let me give you a word of caution here, though: Be certain you get your work done first. Establish reasonable rules with your peers about work related assistance. This will prevent hard feelings later.

There are many events that happen in your day that are relatively unimportant, but somehow they seem more urgent than they really are. We will talk later in the chapter about identifying these time traps and what to do to avoid them.

Emergency

Wouldn't it be wonderful if everything always worked out as we planned? I know you will agree with me when I say, if you believe this you are living a fantasy. Planning your time efficiently can often prevent those emergencies from occurring, but you should invest a few moments thinking of an alternate approach to your most important activities should an emergency arise.

GET ORGANIZED

I have already emphasized the importance of working clean. One of the main causes of wasted time and lost income is disorganization. When you clear your desk, believe it or not, it helps to clear your mind. When your mind is clear, you are more able to focus on one activity or task at a time. And, after all, isn't that all you can accomplish--one thing at a time? Let me make some suggestions to you about how to organize your work space.

First, only keep immediate activities on your desk. All other things should be kept out of sight. Then, keep everything you need to accomplish those immediate tasks near you, so you don't waste steps running here and there.

Secondly, if you are one of those salespeople who suffer from multiple interruptions, take charge. If need be, close your door. If you don't have a door, try ear plugs or a headset attached to a cassette player to isolate yourself. Put in a tape of white noise. Develop your ability to focus intently on your work. Let your staff or family know there are times you are really not to be interrupted. In simple terms, be less accessible. If you need to, set up a certain time of day that your associates know they can freely walk in your office, and other times that are off limits. If they drop by at a bad time, don't be afraid to look at your watch and say, "I'd love to catch up with you, but let's do it at ..." and then name a time later in the day. If what they have to tell you is important enough, they'll be happy to schedule the time. If it's not that important, they'll beg off and you will have saved yourself some time.

Lastly, if the phone is not a necessary tool of your immediate business, remove it from your desk. Put it on a table behind you, or even on the floor if you must--but get it out of your sight. Another thing to remember is, not every phone call is an emergency. When you are on the phone and the other party is getting off the subject or tends to be long-winded, try these techniques.

1. When you initiate the call, tell them "I have three things to cover with you." If they start to get you sidetracked, you then have the right to bring them back to one of your three topics.

2. Call the long-winded party just before lunch time or just before they go home for the day. If that's not possible, start your call by saying, "I'm really pressed for time, but just wanted to let you know ...." Or, "I'm on my way to an appointment...."

If you don't learn to take control in these situations, you'll forever be at the mercy of others and they will hardly ever have your best interests in mind.

Just like the separation of tasks into three categories, you will need to separate your life into three areas in order to effectively organize your time. You will have to investigate your yesterday, analyze your today, and discover your tomorrow through your time management program. Let's begin with yesterday.

Investigate Your Past

Before you can determine where you are going, you must know where you have come from. So, this will be the first step in effective self management. You will need to audit your past. After all, how will you know what you need to improve if you don't take a look at what you have been doing wrong? Remember what we said earlier about memory? It isn't always accurate or unbiased. This is why you must write everything down.

Take some time to write down what you do with the 168 hours in your typical week. If you're like self management beginners, you may have habits that are serious time wasters and can be easily eliminated, once you become aware of them. Try to be as honest and thorough as possible. Keep a daily log for at least 21 days of your typical routine in order to establish an accurate record of habits that may need changing. The best way to do this is to design a customized time sheet. Don't make it so elaborate that you won't complete it each day. Simply jot down the time you spend moving through your daily routine, from the three hours running errands to the five minutes you wasted looking for that purchase agreement or phone message you misplaced.

After completing this time log for 21 days, you'll be amazed at how much time you cannot account for, as well as, how much time is wasted on relatively unimportant activities. Very few of us really know how we spend our time and most of us are surprised at how inaccurate our sense of time is.

The following example is a suggested form you may want to use to begin your 21 day time audit. You may want to customize this to suit your own specific selling needs.

(See following page.)

Today's Work Plan

6		1	
7		2	
8		3	
9		4	
10		5	
11			
12			

#	Top Ten To Do's	☆

Make each block represent an hour of time. Put an X in each block to show you spent a full hour, a slash (/) when you only spent half an hour. If you wish to count the quarter hours, devise a simple system that will be easy to tabulate at the end of your day. Remember, keep it simple and record your time just after each task. Don't try to recreate your time spent at the end of your day. This is not an approximation, but should be as accurate an accounting of your time as possible. If it's one of your goals to exercise for 30 minutes every day, make certain you have a space for that in your log. Include those things that are most important to you on your list. You should record in the note section how you spent your **other** time.

Get tough with yourself. Do this audit for 21 days. After each completed sheet be sure to tally your total hours spent on each category. Keep all your sheets and evaluate them at the end of three weeks. BE HONEST WITH YOUR TIME SPENT.

Remember, this is just a suggested form. If you need to customize your time audit, by all means do so. You know best what needs to be included in your account. Be sure to keep it as simple as possible, while accurately tracking your time.

Analyze Your Today

When you analyze, you break in parts and form a new whole. That is exactly what you will be doing with your today. You have learned from your time log how you have spent your last 21 days. You have seen yesterday's time wasters. You are ready to take apart your today, examine how you can improve it, and put together a new and improved today.

As you discover where you could free up more time for face-to-face selling, you may find a conflict between what you need to do to increase your income, and what the company requires you to do.

TIME PLANNING VS. SELF-MANAGEMENT AND PRODUCTIVITY

In selling you can, in most cases, make the most of your time to make more income. This is not true in a lot of other careers, yet you hear the words 'time planning' applied to sales and 'productivity' to most other careers. I feel salespeople should always use the word productivity when referring to time planning. If they would, time planning would not be such a mystery to them.

Salespeople will frequently come up to me or write to me and say, "Tom, I just can't plan my time" or, "I just can't seem to keep up with everything I need to do." A saying someone gave me when I first started out in selling made a huge impact on my career and my success. It also made a lot of further discussion on the subject unnecessary for me. It goes like this: **I must do the most productive thing possible at every given moment**. I have been teaching that for over 20 years, but it may be so simple that it's not really understood. Let's take a look at what it really means.

Selling is so diverse that trying to teach one time planning system to everyone makes no sense at all. For example, you have inside sales, outside sales, phone sales, etc. Some salespeople have leads furnished, others must do a lot of prospecting to get their leads. Some salespeople deal in large transactions that take many months to complete while others handle small transactions that may take only a few minutes. Some have pre-set appointments. Some set their own. Others just rely on walk-in traffic. Some require great amounts of service after the sale. Others require no service at all. So planning your time is different for almost all of these sales positions. We say that you're not making money in sales if you are not belly to belly with someone who can say "yes" to your product or service, but it's not always true any more and certainly not that simple.

If your company expects you to do a mountain of paperwork on every sale, you have to do it or lose your position with that company. So, you have to consider that productive. Obviously, if you do it at a time when you could be making sales, you are not doing the most productive thing possible at that moment--and that's the true test.

I used to ask myself, and still do, "Is this the most productive thing I can do at this time?" There are a few simple things you need to do to answer that question--such as keeping a list of important tasks to be done, and obviously an appointment calendar. There are also a few others--such as knowing what your time is worth. If you make $40,000 a year, your time (based on a 40 hour week 52 weeks a year) is worth about $19.00 an hour. Now to increase your productivity your challenge is to figure out, by doing the most productive thing at each moment, how to increase the value of each hour. If that sounds simple, it is. Like a lot of things in life, we often contemplate them to a point of utter confusion.

I have seen salespeople spend all their time getting organized and getting ready for a sale that never comes about. To them, getting organized has become the game. Sometimes this happens because a salesperson may be so afraid of facing rejection or failure that they will hide from seeing the public, but in most cases, it's just not having a good understanding of selling and productivity. This is where a good sales manager comes into play. A top sales manager can spot these types of problems and helps the salesperson understand what is happening and gets them on the right path, or recommend a career change.

While we're on the subject of management, let's talk about management styles and how they affect your sales productivity. If you take the premise that most or all of your income comes only when you're in front of and selling customers, then you are probably in a straight commission or a mostly commission sales job. So anything else you're doing can take away from your income--such as attending meetings and filling out paperwork--but both are a fact of life in selling. This is where management style comes into play in a big way in your productivity.

Some companies and sales manager's require an endless stream of paperwork and meetings and wonder why sales are down when in fact, there's little time left to sell. Good sales management will normally not let this happen, but it can sneak up on them a little at a time--a new report accounting wants here, a quick sales meeting there--until your productivity is shot. And it all starts because everyone is trying to do their jobs better. A paperwork person needs paperwork and a manager needs to manage and sometimes they lose sight of the big picture. If you are trying to do the most productive thing possible at every given moment you will spot this trend before anyone else and you should discuss any selling-time challenges it may cause with your manager. Please don't get me wrong here. Paperwork and meetings are valuable to any salesperson and company and should be respected. As a member of the team, you should always do your best to cooperate.

Let's take a quick look at another area. Some sales cycles are longer than others. Let's say you sell a car and deliver it. Other than a few follow-up calls to the customer, you may pretty much complete the sale in a few days.

Let's look at another person who might sell an elaborate computer system. It could take months to sell. Then, you must be involved in delivery and set up and maybe expect to spend a great amount of time making sure the transition to the new equipment is satisfactory to the buyer. Is this productive time? Sure it is. However, if you are on straight commission, you must at the same time be working with new customers in the pipeline. This can obviously be a difficult challenge and calls for good time planning and a thorough understanding of what is the most productive thing for you to do at every given moment.

It would appear to many salespeople that time planning revolves around just buying a time planner and filling in the squares. While that is necessary, it's just a small part of the big picture.

Time planning actually starts with goals. Why? Because that's the only way you can determine what the most productive thing possible at every given moment really is.

Let's take a look at five areas: family, health, financial, spiritual and hobbies. When you are turned on and motivated and feeling good, you can sell better. That should be no shock to anyone. What's this got to do with time planning and productivity? If you let yourself become just a sales machine with no time for anything else, you will eventually burn out. You wiil probably also create problems in your personal relationships. Your health will most likely suffer as well. Besides all that, you will have no fun and in general, get feeling sorry for yourself and your sales career will go down the drain.

Sometimes the most productive thing you can do may be to meet your spouse for lunch in gratitude of supporting your goals and putting up with the long hours, or go to see your child in a school event to lessen your guilt and enjoy their childhood, or take a physical workout to help insure your good health and high energy. Or, it may be productive to plant roses if that's your hobby. To be successful in sales you need to be a finely tuned machine that can function over the long haul and face deadlines, rejection, the public and your competition. You must also be able to meet your company's expectations and all the other demands put on you as a professional salesperson and problem-solver. You must keep that

machine tuned and in balance and this balance starts with goals and productivity.

Let's assume your goals and priorities are in line and you know what
you want and how you want to get there. Your goals are all in writing and
your priorities are set. I believe your daily time planning should start at
night before you go to bed. Go through your time planner and lay out the
day. Get a handle on your top ten priorities, as well as who you will see
or call. Then also add in any personal areas you need to cover that day.
This shouldn't take more than 10-15 minutes maximum if you do it in a
nice, quiet spot. <u>Once you do it, forget it and go to bed</u>.

The next day the most productive thing possible may start at 6:00 a.m.
with a 20-minute workout or breakfast with the family or working in the
garden or 1,000 other things that are important to you and are part of your
goals and priorities. It goes the same way through the entire day. You
have a lot of choices. Only you know if what you are doing is the most
productive thing in relation to the goals and aspirations you want to
achieve.

**In sales, if you make too many bad choices in your priorities you
may soon be looking for a job where someone will tell you what to do
all day.** Some people can't make the tough time planning and productivity choices to make the money they want from selling. Anyone who's been
in selling for a few years will tell you that it's no big secret. Selling takes
some guts to make tough personal choices. If you can do it you will have
the great rewards. If you can't, you languish and leave sales and blame
everything and everyone but yourself. Another bottom line truth is that
all of us grow up being told what to do for as much as the first 20 years of
our lives--at home, then at school, then on a job--so it's not surprising that
we lack a certain amount of self-discipline when we go into a career
where we are left to our own resources. I would like to have a dollar for
every time I have heard a salesperson say, "I went into sales so I could be
my own boss" or, "I went into sales so no one would tell me what to do"
or, "I went into sales for more free time." All those reasons are great, but
they better develop a strong degree of self-discipline to do what needs to
be done or they will soon be back at a job where someone's telling them
what to do.

Ready-Set-Plan

To get started with an effective time management method, don't try to plan for every minute of the day, because most of us are often inaccurate when forecasting time for task completion. Begin by planning just 75% of your total work time to allow for interruptions, delays, and those unexpected emergencies. As you become better at effectively planning your workday, you can build to planning 90% of your day. If you try to plan for 100%, you're not allowing for the unexpected, and you will frustrate yourself when you cannot accomplish your designated tasks.

Another important factor is to remain flexible. Nothing is truly black or white; there are also gray areas. By staying flexible, you are able to maintain your equilibrium and move on to greater things. Don't lock yourself into a time management program so rigid that you don't have time for anything else.

Top salespeople always plan their time. To increase your sales and your income, you must plan your time too. A Champion salesperson is very conscious of the value of their customer's time, as well as their own. All sales professionals are forced to make daily decisions on priorities. Some are major, some are minor, but all are factors in the management of time. Every professional salesperson needs a systematic approach to setting their priorities.

Over the years I've noticed that very successful people who run large companies and build fortunes, really don't spend much more time working than anyone else. The difference is that very successful people have the ability to get more productivity out of each hour of every day. They don't try to do too much at once and, because of this, are more productive at the six most important things they need to do.

That is where I want you to begin to focus on discovering your tomorrows. Don't be intimidated, it's really quite simple. The end result of time planning can be the best source of increased income that you will ever develop.

USING A TIME PLANNER

Find some type of planning notebook that works for you. It's especially helpful if you can customize it. Day Timers® of Allentown,

Pennsylvania has a wonderful line of useful planning and organizing products that I myself have used for 25 years, that can help you to increase your personal productivity.

Some suggestions for using your time planner:

1. Always write your name, business address and phone number on it, in case you leave it somewhere.

2. Write down your long and short term goals in it so you will be reminded of them on a daily basis.

3. Place a check mark in the "done" box when you have completed something or cross it off.

4. Write appointments down as soon as possible. Allow for travel time when scheduling around them.

5. Plan your **ten** most important things you must do first.

6. Schedule your most important tasks or customers when you are at your physical and mental peak. Some people are at their best in the morning. They begin the day full of boundless energy and then become less energetic as the day progresses. Others are slow starting out but then blast off and finish the day strong.

7. When scheduling any activity, estimate the time it will take, and then add another 20%.

8. Expect the unexpected.

9. Always keep your yearly calendar updated with major events such as birthdays, anniversaries, conventions, meetings, etc.

When to Plan

On the first day of every month, sit down with your planning notebook and write down everything you want to accomplish this month. Be realistic in what you write down. Write down any family or social events you are committed to, first. Then, write down any important dates like family and client birthdays, your anniversary, special events, such as your child's school play, etc. If you've promised to be somewhere for your children or your spouse, write it down so you can plan around it.

The next thing is to note all the company meetings you must attend for the month. And then add any projects you are working on, estimated completion dates, and follow-up notes. If you are working on a large project, try to break it down into smaller pieces you can accomplish each week. This will help you to see the progress and it won't seem so oppressive.

In daily time planning, keep track of all activities as you go. Don't wait until 4 p.m. to try to remember what you did at 9:30 a.m. Be truthful, don't play around with numbers or fake anything just to check it off.

Questions to Ask Yourself When Analyzing Your Daily Time Planner:

1. Did I reach or surpass my sales goals for today?
2. Did I invest as much time as I planned in face-to-face selling?
3. Did I contact every prospect that I had on my list for today? If not, why not? What prevented me from getting to that prospect?
4. How much time did I spend prospecting for new clients?
5. How much time did I waste chatting with co-workers or clients who are "friendly time-wasters"?
6. What is the most productive thing I did today?
7. What is the least productive thing I did today?
8. Of the things that I feel were a waste of time, could they have been avoided or eliminated?
9. How much time did I spend doing something that will result profitably? Can I devote more time here?
10. Did I accomplish all ten of my high priority items?
11. Was today a productive day for me? For my company?
12. Did I take care of all the paperwork I needed today?
13. How many of today's activities have helped me toward the achievement of my goals?
14. How much time today did I allot to my family? Did I spend this time with them? Was it quality time or were we just in the house at the same time?
15. What can I do to improve the quality of the time I have devoted to my family?
16. Did I plan for, and take some time to work on my emotional or physical health?
17. If I could live today over, what would I change?

18. What did I do today that I feel really good about?
19. Did I send thank you notes to the people I dealt with today?
20. What or who wasted the greatest amount of my time?

COMMON TIME TRAPS

Every profession has a few time wasting aspects and every relationship has a degree of wasted energy. But, let's take a look at the greatest time wasters in professional sales:

1. Disorganization

A sure way to waste valuable time is to spend it looking for something you need because you were careless with it. This is the single biggest time waster for everyone. How many hours have you wasted in your career looking for that one scrap of paper you wrote a customer's phone number on, or that folder with all the referrals that your new client gave you? How about your sunglasses or your car keys? Ring any bells? Those few minutes here and there can really add up.

2. Failure to Do the Job Right the First Time

Because of the demands we place on ourselves, we tend to rush through planning presentations and paperwork without carefully checking or re-checking details. There's a saying that goes, "If you don't have time to do it right the first time, how will you find time to do it again?" Consider how much less time it takes to do something right the first time, than to go back and do it over. The professional salesperson doesn't risk angering his/her clients with costly delays or mistakes caused by carelessly written orders. Pros double-check everything for accuracy and clarity.

3. Procrastination

Procrastination and sales call reluctance can be fatal to a selling career. Don't feel alone on this one, everyone procrastinates. We all tend to put things off until we create a "have to" situation. Most people procrastinate because of fear. They fear making a mistake, so instead they do nothing. The trouble with doing nothing is this: it can only produce nothing. Mistakes can, and will, happen many times in each of our lives. We need to accept the mistakes and learn from our past experiences. Another reason to procrastinate is anxiety. The best way to overcome procrastination is to develop a plan and then follow it.

If a client phones and has a problem with the product or service, what do most people do? They put it off until tomorrow and then when they call to apologize and solve the problem, the client may be furious and vowing to never do business with them again. Always call an angry client immediately. The longer you wait, the worse it will become. Perhaps you've heard the saying, "A professional is someone who does things even when they don't want to." How true. It takes discipline. To be truly successful, overcome procrastination. Procrastination leads to immobilization which is the biggest killer of all selling careers. Words to live by: DO IT NOW!!!

4.   Unnecessary or Unnecessarily Long Phone Calls
A real problem for many business people. The telephone can be a salesperson's greatest ally or greatest enemy. Here are some ideas to help you deal with wasted time on the phone:
   a) Set aside specific time each day to take and make phone calls.
   b) Set a time limit for your calls.
   c) Write down your objective for the phone call and focus on it.
   d) Have all your materials and information readily available to you before you pick up the phone.
   e) Decide on a specific time limit on all calls.
   f) Develop phraseology to help you get off the phone without interrupting the other person, or abruptly ending the conversation. For instance, try saying: "Barbara, just one more thing before we hang up..." This lets the person know that you are coming to the end of the phone call.
   g) Let all your customers know exactly when you are available to be contacted by phone.
   h) If you do business with people who chatter and won't let you off the phone, when they call tell them you're in the middle of some

thing extremely urgent and that you will call them back. Then, call them just before the time they leave for the day. You'll be surprised how brief these conversations can suddenly become.

i)   If you spend great amounts of time on the phone, or are in tele-marketing, a high-quality headset will be a valuable investment for you.

5.   Unnecessary or Unnecessarily Long Meetings

Attending too many nonproductive meetings can also be a major time waster for salespeople. If you're in management and you feel that a great deal of your time is wasted in meetings, perhaps you should re-evaluate how often you need to meet with your employees and what you need to accomplish when you do assemble. Is a daily or weekly meeting necessary or can more effective communications within the company eliminate the need for such meetings? Don't hold a $1,000 meeting to solve a $50 problem. Many people have found that holding meetings standing up is highly productive. People don't settle into comfortable chairs for the duration and get finished much more quickly. Some companies have actually started a policy of holding short meetings standing up. That's not a bad idea.

6.   Client Lunches that Last for Two or More Hours

As with the phone, you need to develop ways to let the client know that you have finished your business for today and must move on. For instance, when you sit down for lunch at noon with a notorious "friendly afternoon waster", you could say something to the effect of: "This works out great. I don't have another commitment until 1:30, so we have plenty of time to talk."

7.   Negative Thinking

Negative thoughts that produce negative talk are the biggest waste of time for everyone. If you think and dwell on life's negatives, what do you think you can accomplish? I'm positive you will accomplish very little. Push negative thoughts from your mind. No one ever became a success who was a negative thinker. Instead of focusing on things you don't like, think about the positive things you can do. Another helpful hint is to surround yourself with positive thinkers. It will amaze you how their positive energy will rub off on you.

8. Driving Time

Most people in professional selling spend a lot of time in their cars driving from appointment to appointment. The average salesperson drives 25,000 miles a year for their job. That works out to about 500 hours, which is about 12 1/2 weeks. This is your basic college semester.

How can you make the best use of this time? Like I have said before, I teach my students that education should be a continuous journey. A true professional is the person who keeps learning, after they know it all. Why not invest this time in your education? You have to allow time in your day for the travel time to and from your clients, so make a commitment to use this time to expand your mind.

There are hundreds of educational programs available on cassette. Publishing companies recorded books on cassettes because people today don't always have the time to sit down and read a book. You can use this driving time to listen to programs on sales training, motivation, self-esteem, financial planning, small business strategies, foreign language, classic literature, history, as well as, an enormous number of "How To" programs. Every one of us need to keep learning as long as there is something that we don't know.

Another consideration to make the best use of driving time is to carefully plan your calls, as I pointed out before. One of the biggest time wasters is poor planning of sales calls in a geographic area. Again, learn to cluster your sales calls. Don't drive back and forth across town each week, group calls on one side of town one day, then cover the other side the next day.

9. Unconfirmed Appointments

It amazes me how many salespeople do not confirm appointments before they leave the office or the previous customer. Why would anyone do this? Again, FEAR. We're afraid that if we call, they might say, "Never mind." We'd rather drive all the way to their office and have the receptionist tell us they were called out of town for the day. A quick phone call before you leave not only can save you valuable selling time, it tells the prospect that you are a professional with something valuable to say.

If handled properly, your brief call to confirm could just possibly keep your appointment from being the one that gets canceled if there's a need to make changes in that decision-maker's schedule. When calling to confirm an appointment, do it this way: "Hi, Jim, I have spent so much time preparing for our meeting and I just thought I'd call to let you know I'll be there right at 2:00. I think you'll be excited about what I have to show you." Never say, "I'm just calling to confirm." By letting him or her know how much time and effort you put into preparing for this meeting, they'll feel guilty about cancelling and be more likely to find a way to keep the appointment. If, for some reason you can't get to the person you have the appointment with, tell the person taking the message that you are on your way and will be on time. Ask that they get that message to the customer you are meeting with.

Another benefit would be that even if they do have to cancel, you have them on the phone to immediately schedule another appointment. Always take the time to confirm your appointments. The time you save will be well worth it. It will free up your time to prospect for new business or to take care of something else on your list.

10. Television

In my experience with people who are high achievers, almost every one of them will tell you that they do not waste time watching television. I'm not going to preach to you the mindlessness of the majority of what we see on TV these days, but I will just say that TV should be used properly. I believe TV is the single least productive activity in the American lifestyle.

Learn to Say No

Many of us can't say no when people want a chunk of our time, however, it is better that we say no to someone, than to say yes and not get the job done. Believe me when I say, saying no in these circumstances is caring enough for the person to want the best possible job done for them. If your saying yes means they stop looking for someone to help them do the job, and you fail to do what you said you would, you have hurt them more than saying no in the beginning would have done.

Sometimes you are really not the one most capable to do the job in the first place. Professionals recognize their limitations and learn to delegate these requests to those who are more capable, and more likely to complete the job in an efficient manner. If this is explained properly, with warmth and caring, those asking you for favors will appreciate your honesty and ability to refer them to someone trustworthy to do the job. As you become more successful, your time will become more valuable, so learn when you need to say no.

Solo Time

While you should always allow part of your day to work with people, support your co-workers, or help the company problem-solve, it is also important that you allow for some solo time at work and in your personal life. This is time that is for whatever you need to do. This can be your time for emotional and physical health in your private life, as well as, your most productive work time.

During your solo work time, if someone says, "Do you have a minute?" Simply answer, "Not right now. Can it wait until eleven?" By that time, most people who were looking for your help will have solved the problem themselves or didn't have anything that was of great importance anyway.

Some tips for handling interruptions:

1. Rearrange your office so your desk is out of the line of sight from people walking down the hallway.

2. Remove extra chairs from your office if possible. Position any necessary chairs as far away from your desk as possible.

3. Place a large clock where you and your visitor can clearly see it.

4. When someone walks into your office, don't look up. This is difficult to do at first, but if you appear to be extremely busy and it's nothing serious, most people will simply walk away. This may sound a bit cold, but if you can't get your work done, it's going to cause your customers to receive less service and you to receive a lower income. Beware, there are people in every company who just like to walk around and visit.

To get started on minimizing this problem, keep an Interruption Log. In it write:

1. Who is interrupting you?
2. What time they came and left.
3. How much time was wasted?
4. What can you do about it?

When an occasional crisis comes up, deal with it quickly and then go back to your original schedule immediately. I'm not suggesting that you become anti-social in your office, but I am saying that you may be surprised at how much more efficient you can be when you begin to take back those minutes here and there.

High Tech Time Savers

The rapid advancement of technology is the salesperson's friend. Many new products have become available lately that do so much to save you time.

Back in my selling days, we had to write down and keep track of an incredible amount of information. Who could have imagined back then that in 25 years there would be computers that you could not only move from place to place easily, but they would be smaller than a briefcase and fit comfortably on your lap giving you instant access to all your files and information? Who could have imagined that if you needed to get in touch with someone on an airplane at 37,000 feet, that you could just pick up the phone and call them? Who could have imagined that you could get a letter from Los Angeles to New York in under two minutes, via a FAX machine?

The Outside Salesperson's Best Friend

If you don't invest in anything else for your success, get a car phone or portable phone. I can't imagine anyone in outside sales who wouldn't benefit greatly from this important time saver. If you don't own one now, get one. It will more than pay for itself in the greater income you will earn due to the higher quality of service you are able to give your customers.

Better yet, get a mobile phone that you can keep with you at all times. With a mobile phone, your office can always reach you if a customer has a problem or if a prospect you've been working with calls and has decided that he/she is ready to do business with you.

Another important tool for many of today's outside salespeople is a portable fax machine. If you need vital paperwork while you are in the field, I can think of no better piece of equipment to have than the portable fax.

Some Suggestions for High-Tech Tools

One thing to remember about mobile phones is to use proper business etiquette. Never take one into a presentation with you that is turned on unless you and the customer are waiting for an important call regarding that particular meeting. If your phone rings in the middle of the presentation and you stop to take the call, how do you think the prospect will react to that? If you were considering investing a good amount of money in a product and the salesperson stopped their presentation to take a call, wouldn't you feel that the salesperson was rude to ignore you while they spoke with someone else? Would you say yes to someone who wasted your valuable time? The same with beepers, put it on "vibrate" or turn it off when you are with a prospect.

When using a FAX machine, always use a cover sheet with all your business numbers and then take a minute to call the recipient and make sure they have received the fax. Be certain to tell them how many pages you sent. Many companies, with hundreds of employees, have just one FAX machine. It would be easy for your fax to be misplaced. It could even get batched in with another fax that came in previously and given to the wrong person who may not realize they have it until much later. Even in small offices, a fax can get buried under other papers. Take a moment to call. This will show the prospect that you are a caring professional.

PAPERWORK

If you dread doing the paperwork, don't leave it for the end of the day if you can help it. Should something unexpected come up, you don't get to it, and the next day you have twice as much to do. This in turn, causes you even more anxiety because now you really have a big task ahead of you. Do your paperwork in the first hour if at all possible when you are freshest. Once it's done, you are free to concentrate on the more productive parts of your day.

We have spent, or rather invested, a lot of time in this chapter to teach you to make every hour count. I hope you will go back over this material from time to time and review it. Auditing your time is not just a one time event. You should practice periodical 2-3 day time audits at least every 90 days. This will keep you on track. The best advice I can give anyone about managing their time is to live by these words:

I MUST DO
THE MOST PRODUCTIVE THING POSSIBLE
AT EVERY GIVEN MOMENT!

CHAPTER 9
CREATING A POSITIVE OUTLOOK
AND HIGH SELF-ESTEEM

I have been involved in selling for over 25 years. During that time, I have witnessed many careers devastated because the salespeople were unable to believe in their potential for success. They were sabotaging themselves through faulty information they were feeding their minds. They had low, poor or negative self-esteem. In this chapter, I hope to help you realize if you are doing the same thing to yourself and how to overcome it.

What Is Self-Esteem?
Simplified, it's what you think about yourself -- your opinion of you. It's a compiled reflection of what you believe to be true about you in every aspect of your life, in every situation you encounter.

Let's say you believe yourself to be a good person overall and on a 1 to 10 scale you give yourself a rating of 8. You admit there are some areas in which you could improve. That 8 is an average of all the aspects of your life that are important to you. It includes how you see yourself as a child, a sibling, a spouse, friend, student, sales professional, athlete, driver, businessperson, investor, hobbyist, etc.

The important thing to realize is that your opinion of yourself in each of those areas dictates how you act in every situation you encounter. And even more importantly, your opinion can and will change with every experience you have. The best news of all is that you have the ability to alter your perspective and the way you feel about yourself. In fact, you are the only one who can choose how you think about yourself.

You may be wondering about some of the areas in your life that may not be so positive. Surely, you wouldn't choose to let a negative perspective develop, would you? The programming begins at birth and then we have little control over how we react to it. However, later in life negative self-esteem may develop by default -- by simply failing to exercise control over what goes into your mind.

What about those famous sayings we've all heard (or maybe even said) such as, "It's my nature. I've always been that way. That's just me. I was raised that way. I've always done it this way." You may not like what I'm going to say next, but these sayings are nothing but cop outs, excuses or justifications we come up with for not doing as well at something as we think we should or as someone else thinks.

Trust me, low self-esteem can be a real drain not only on your career, but on every aspect of your life. Soon you will be telling yourself, "Oh, what's the use. I'm just wasting my time." You are defeating yourself before you ever meet face-to-face with a customer, and unfortunately, customers will sense your defeated attitude before you even open your mouth. Your entire manner is effected by poor self-esteem.

For some of you reading this book, this information may be the seed of awakening. It can bring a realization that breaks the chains of limitation you have put on yourself. If that's the case, get ready for some excitement. Once you truly understand that you and you alone can choose how you will respond to life's crises and challenges, dramatic changes can and will happen in your life.

If you were given the talent to create something that will influence every aspect of your life, you would want to use that talent with care, wouldn't you? Think about your life right now. In fact, I recommend that you take a few moments with a lined pad of paper and list all the aspects of your life that are truly important to you -- being a good spouse, an involved parent, a good tennis player or whatever. Then, rate yourself in each area on a 1 to 10 scale. Don't take too much time to think about it. Just write down the number that comes to mind right away.

Once you've completed the list, go back and write down the rating you would like to have in each area. Now, close your eyes for a moment and realize how you would feel if you achieved your desired rating in every aspect of your life. Feels wonderful, doesn't it? Now, hold onto that feeling and believe me when I say that you have the ability to achieve those higher ratings. You can change. You can become a better person in all areas of your life.

Now, let's talk about self-esteem and how it relates to the main topic of our book -- sales. How does your current image of yourself as a salesperson affect what you do each and every day in selling? Your picture of yourself as a salesperson will dictate how much money you will earn, which in turn dictates the lifestyle you will have.

If you have a poor image of yourself in sales, you will see yourself as being inadequate. Because of your negative attitude, you will act inadequately. Because of your actions, others will believe you to be inadequate and your sales figures will show it.

Now, please understand that while it's important for you to raise your self-esteem, attitude is not enough. You must act like those people whose incomes prove they are at the level you desire. Often, that will involve a certain degree of work. You will have to be willing to read the books a person at that level would read. Attend seminars those people would attend. Practice, drill and rehearse your presentations as someone at that rating would. Then, your sales will increase. Your income level will increase and your new perspective will direct you to continue performing at that higher rate because you have now proven yourself to be at that level.

Allowing yourself to think negatively can be compared to parenting. You certainly wouldn't let your child be exposed to any unnecessary risk, if you could stop it, would you? Then, why let it happen to you? By harnessing the power in controlling your thoughts, you can achieve greatness in whatever you set your goals for.

Having a strong, positive attitude in sales will help you turn the negatives that are a normal part of the business into learning experiences that will make you even stronger in the future.

Emulate a Model for Success

Whether we realize it or not, every one of us has someone we look up to and admire. We humans need this. We are constantly choosing people we wish to be like through the clothing we wear, the cars we drive, even the food we eat and type of exercise we get. Billions of dollars are invested in advertising each year to show us what the people we want to be like are thinking and doing. If we do what they do, we'll be as successful, beautiful, popular, or whatever as they are.

When you choose someone to emulate in your selling career or business, you must grow to believe that you are capable of achieving the same success. Use them as a measurement to gauge your progress. You may surprise yourself and surpass their achievements in no time. Soon you will be the model for some other up and coming sales professional. It is really a wonderful chain of events.

That is exactly what happened to me in my journey to success. I chose J. Douglas Edwards to be my model. To me, he epitomized the true professional. Even though Mr. Edwards became a strong role model for me, I soon trusted my own instincts and developed sales techniques and skills above and beyond what I learned from him.

Remember, those people you hold in high regard are always changing, too. They may have their own role models and be working to achieve even greater things in their lives. Eventually, you may grow to become very much like your role models or even exceed their achievements. That's when you get busy and choose another model.

This is a good time to go back to your personal inventory and choose a model for each category. Look at what you would need to do to be more like them. Now go back, using the inventory as a guide, and list several things you can do to improve in each area. By putting your personal goals in writing, you are on your way to improving yourself as well as your sales results.

Don't try to change everything at once, you will be too overwhelmed. Take one thing at a time and work on it until you become satisfied with your results. Then move to the next category. The more involved and enthusiastic you become when improving your perspective, the more likely you are to continually improve. You see, it's those feelings that create the fuel for change. Even very small changes in each area raise self-esteem because they make you feel good and positive about yourself.

Imagination vs. Reality

Think about the ability your imagination has to affect your personality and behavior. If your perspective is realistic, you are almost limitless as to what you can achieve. Sure your capabilities can be improved, but if you don't picture your improved self, you will continue making the same old mistakes. You must first imagine or develop a higher self-esteem, then you will fully benefit from your further education. Focus on controlling and improving those things that can be controlled, and stop dwelling on those things you now believe impossible to change or that you have no control over. By continuing to dwell on them, you are wasting precious energy that could be put to better use.

Have you ever wondered why many people can attend the same sales seminar but not take with them the same information that will lead them to success? They all heard the same message. They all invested the same amount of time at the seminar. They all were interested in improving their selling skills and techniques. So, why do some achieve greatness, while others seem to stay in the same old rut? Is it because some are more intelligent than others? Perhaps. Or, maybe some want it more and work harder to achieve it? Could be.

While those can be factors that contribute to the professional's success, I say what makes the difference is more than their intelligence, or even their desire. What makes Champions? It is their positive outlook and belief in themselves as Champions. They see themselves as Champions and do what Champions do.

The Champion's boundaries are established just like your boundaries--through their own perspective. The difference is that they don't limit themselves by the constant feeding of negative or inadequate information. I don't just mean positive thinking. I mean positive actions to go along with it.

I truly believe humans are created to improve all the time. Why? Because we can and if we aren't, we get frustrated and bored. We have all experienced the wonderful light feeling that comes from doing something we enjoy. Time seems to fly by and our energy stays high hour after hour. Whatever you like to do that gives you that feeling, try to build on it and carry it over into other areas of your life.

Here is what I did that worked for me. I always loved that warm feeling I got when someone helped me with something I was doing. I hope you know what I mean. I'm referring to someone you knew cared about you -- a teacher, mom, dad or a friend. They helped you with a project or some other task. I noticed I got that same feeling when I helped someone else where I really felt I made a difference. I tried to give that feeling of genuine concern to my customers and at the same time I receive a feeling of appreciation from them.

When I first got into sales, this didn't work. Everyone loved me, but my family and I weren't doing very well. I felt great and my self-esteem was wonderful in the area of helping others, but my esteem in the area of providing income for my family was at rock bottom. As I told you in Chapter 1, I was introduced to sales training and I knew then I could help my customers better. So, I made the pursuit of sales knowledge and the words, feelings and actions that go into sales, my hobby. To this day, I love to watch and listen to all kinds of sales presentations. When I was finally able to combine the feelings I described earlier with hard work and dedication, a sales star was born. My self-esteem, or self-worth, seemed to rise with my net worth. It was truly amazing. I was having a great time helping people get into homes and making a great living for my family. I also found a great hobby -- all within just a few months.

That year, I was so afraid it would all end that I read every book on selling I could find. I read about marketing, goal setting and anything else I could find that I thought related to my sales career and could help me serve my buyers and sellers. As I got better, my sales volume got bigger. I actually had to get help with my paperwork so I could do what I did best, which was one-on-one interaction with my customers.

My greatest gift to your self-esteem would be somehow with your product or service to make this story your story. I hope you will learn to love and study selling as much as I do. It will help you move to a higher plane in your career. Guaranteed! What the heck, if you are gong to be in selling, get your toes out of the water and dive in! The water is great if you are in for the right reasons and put your customer's needs first. Please understand that when you love what you do, you can get carried away sometimes. Don't you agree?

In emulating a role model, remember, that you must do more than change how you appear on the outside. You must also emulate their desire, values and other internal qualities if you wish to achieve what they have achieved. You'll need to gain an understanding of why they do what they do, what their goals are, how sincere and empathetic they are, etc.

The first step is in recognizing you may have some false attitudes about yourself. How do you know if your picture of yourself is correct? Ask yourself these questions to help you decide.

1. What are the reasons I believe the things about myself that I do?
2. Are these reasons sound? Why or why not? (Get very specific here. Come up with specific examples.)
3. Do I know anyone who looks or acts much like me who is very successful? Does this prove that some of my information about myself may be incorrect?
4. If there are others who act and look much like myself and are very successful, why should I continue to believe these false ideas about myself?
5. What can I do to change my perspective and feelings about myself?

Give yourself time to look over your answers to these questions. Don't just glance over them. Study them. Discover new truths about yourself. Now you are on the road to recovering your true perspective and improving your sales too.

Now let's take a look at when you first developed the perspective you have. The mental pictures we develop of ourselves originate at a very, very young age. Once you accept something as truth, it is fed into your mind and used to support your perspective, even when the information is wrong.

As an adult, chances are you are carrying some incorrect reflections of yourself that were given to you as a young person, and you accepted it as truth. For example, many people think they are bad when it comes to

math. Somewhere along the way, they were told this and they accepted it
as truth. By accepting it as truth, their behavior supported this perspective.

CHOOSE TO CHANGE

If you want to change your perspective, **act as if you already have**.
Act as if you are that positive, successful Champion. Remember, your
mind cannot distinguish between what is real and what you imagine to be
real. So, fool yourself for a while. You will build an attitude that you are
a professional salesperson, and eventually, you will become one, but don't
forget the work and study part.

Let me give you an illustration. Have you ever left for an appointment
in a grumpy, cranky mood? You know you cannot give your presentation
with this sort of attitude. So as soon as you get to the door, you put on a
cheery face. You smile at your customers and what do they do? They
smile back. They aren't aware of your earlier grumpiness, so they believe
you to be an up, positive person. Throughout your presentation, the feedback you get from your customers is warm and genuine, and soon the arti-
ficial smile that you wore as you entered their home, is now warm and
genuine too. By acting as if you were happy, you became so.

Is it always that simple? It can be if we allow it to be. The trouble is
most of us won't let go and act "as if" that easily. Especially in sales.
Many salespeople focus on all the negatives they received yesterday,
instead of believing this presentation to be a positive experience today.

Even during your busiest day, you can only experience one moment at
a time. This being true, you can only successfully complete one task at a
time too. If you take each task as a new and different experience and
refuse to allow yourself to be affected by past failures, you will be feeding
successful behavior and attitudes into your mind to develop a successful
self-esteem.

How Important are Habits to Our Behavior?

You can't change your self-esteem just by thinking and examining all
the information you see and hear. Reading this book can't really change it

either. Your family and friends telling you what a terrific person you are can't really change your self-esteem. So what can? What changes your perspective is your own attitude, belief, knowledge and experiences.

Champion salespeople are not just those who have attended all the seminars and read all the books available to them. They are the salespeople who have taken the information they have learned combined with a positive attitude about themselves, and gone on to **experience** their own success.

Now what do our habits have to do with our success? If you consistently establish productive habits, you allow yourself more successful experiences to support the level of self-esteem you are developing every day. Remember, this process should be in constant change. Why? Because of your daily experiences. If you want to change an attitude, it usually takes about 21 days of changed behavior, thinking, and imagining to make it a reality for you. So, be patient.

It is surprising how soon you will begin to realize what you are becoming through these new habits. Form strong positive behavioral habits as a foundation to build your new level of self-esteem. Earlier we spoke of how it often just takes one negative to wipe out many positives. Well, this is true with habits also. You may have established many productive habits to build a foundation for success, but the power of one bad habit can cause cracks in that structure.

If your bad habit goes uncorrected, those cracks in the foundation may become huge fissures, letting in self-doubt that can lead to an incorrect perspective. So, form the habit of reacting positively to people who may threaten your success. Don't give them power or influence over your life. Form the habit of planning future goals, but remain grounded in the present. It is important to see and believe in your success NOW. If this is difficult for you, write these statements on a small card and keep it in front of you all day. Don't just pay lip service to these affirmations. It's the feelings behind the words that give them power. If, after a while, the affirmations become empty phrases, it is time to change them to ones that are backed by strong feelings and emotions. Here are some examples to help you get started. Once you get the idea, you'll make up your own affirmations that will be even more powerful.

1. I am a professional salesperson.
2. I am constantly working toward achieving my planned goals.
3. I am an optimistic thinker.
4. I react calmly and intelligently to critical situations.
5. I am a powerhouse of positive emotions and feelings.

What does the word habit really mean? It originally meant a garment or a piece of clothing. This gives us some insight on the effectiveness of successful habits. First of all, we are always going to have them--good or bad. We have them for a purpose. Like clothing, habits provide a covering for our personalities. Make your habits suit you. Constantly develop new and improved habits when you grow out of your old habits that don't fit your present self. The best part of that definition is the mental picture it gives us of something that can be changed. Imagine -- your bad habits can be changed as easily as changing your clothing. For most of us, it's just a matter of being able to decide what else to 'wear.'

Here is an interesting statistic to keep in mind. Did you know that 95% of everything you do and feel is habitual? Do you realize what this means? If necessary, you are capable of changing approximately 95% of those things that most contribute to your perspective. Isn't it encouraging to know that you don't have to be pushed around by that false perspective any longer? JUST CHANGE IT.

Think Pleasant Thoughts

Talk about a powerful tool. It sounds simple, so why do we make it difficult? The principles of P.M.A. or having a Positive Mental Attitude have been taught for years. To simplify them, consider this: We are all carrying on conversations with ourselves every waking moment. We can direct those conversations either in a positive or negative manner. It takes just as much effort to do either, so why not think positive thoughts and carry on positive conversations with ourselves? If you're not already consciously directing your thoughts, it will take some effort to change the way you're thinking now. However, once you've accomplished that change, the constant positive flow of thoughts will become natural to you and your life will change dramatically.

Research has been done on people who make a habit of thinking positively. You may have guessed that not only does it affect your mental well-being, but your physical self is improved also. During the testing period, when people had pleasant thoughts they experienced heightened senses. They could see, taste, smell, hear, and feel slight differences in touch better. Think about how this could really improve your sales.

If one of the most important things during a sales presentation is to be more aware of yourself and your customers, wouldn't you be better prepared to observe behaviors if you were thinking positively? I'm sure you are all familiar with the "What if" game. You know, when you ask yourself before the presentation, "What if the customer gets angry and throws me out on my ear?" Wouldn't it be just as easy to think positively before that presentation and ask yourself, "What if the customer gets so involved with my product or service they not only want to own it, but they recommend me to three other business associates who need my product too?" Now that's what I call productive use of your imagination. It certainly gives you the edge in your sales career.

Now let's look at the affect your new perspective can have on your energy level. For example, how many of you have left a successful presentation where you believed yourself to be the power behind making the sale? First, you had to gain the customer's trust and faith in both you and your product, and you did so with finesse. Then you had to overcome multiple objections, and you were able to do so with complete confidence that they would be well satisfied. You finally consummated the sale. In other words, they bought you and your product or service.

Even though the presentation may have lasted for hours, you came away from it feeling like you could run a twenty-six mile marathon. Why? Because you believed yourself to be a successful professional, and you proved your positive attitude about yourself to be correct. What a rush! This feeling is better than any substance high, and it makes you a good living to boot.

Now let's look at the flip side. When you have worked hard on a presentation, but it just didn't turn out as planned, how is your energy level when you leave? You leave your customer with your feet dragging and your mind weary. It's likely that you'll then drain yourself of whatever energy you have left by dwelling on what went wrong.

A great number of people have felt inferior at some point in their lives. In fact, the majority of the human population has probably let their inferior feelings determine their level of self-esteem. What a shame. Look at it this way. If the most successful salespeople you have heard of or known wanted to feel inferior, they could search for someone who was more successful than they are. So isn't everyone inferior to someone?

When it is difficult to let go of a negative is when it greatly influences your picture or perception. If I might refer to Maxwell Maltz once again, I will illustrate to you what he considers to be a "Success Type" and a "Failure Type" perspective.

A Picture of the Success Type Perspective

S ense of Direction	These people look forward to accomplishing their planned goals.
U nderstanding	These people see the true nature of their problem. They are able to be honest with others and themselves.
C ourage	These people have the boldness to ACT on their decisions. They turn their dreams into realities.
C harity	These people care for and respect others as well as themselves.
E steem	These people hold a realistically high opinion of self.
S elf-Confident	These people learn from their past experiences and then forget about them.
S elf Acceptance	These people truly like themselves.

A Picture of the Failure Type Perspective

F rustration	These people do not realize that all desires cannot be satisfied immediately. They often set unrealistic goals.
A ggressiveness	These people often compare themselves to others they see as ideally successful. The

problem with this is no one really knows another's private thoughts. What is success to one might be failure to another. Making these comparisons can be very unfair to yourself and the one you compare yourself with.

I <u>nsecurity</u>   These people imagine themselves to be inadequate. They sometimes imagine others reactions to them are negative too.

L <u>oneliness</u>   These people are isolated from life. They do this because they wish to decrease their feelings of inferiority. Instead they do just the opposite.

U <u>ncertainty</u>   These people have not learned to trust their decisions.

R <u>esentment</u>   These people always blame others for their failures. They give others a great deal of power over them.

E <u>mptiness</u>   These people always postpone their happiness until they can measure up to some ideal self. Remember to enjoy the journey.

If you look for happiness in tomorrow, you will miss it today. So, get into the happiness habit. It is our constitutional right. We have the right to achieve sales success during our pursuit of happiness. Don't think of it as a selfish act--to make yourself happy. Think of all the wonderful opportunities you will be helping your customers experience if you are happily involved in your own sales career. After all, if you cannot make yourself happy there is little chance of you contributing to another's happiness either.

Key to Success

Even though working hard, learning as much as possible about your career, achieving your planned goals, and helping others to achieve their goals is important--that which makes this all possible is maintaining a healthy, positive, realistic self-esteem. If you practice those things talked about in this chapter, and practice them for at least 21 days consecutively, you will see wonderful changes in your behavior and your level of success.

Remember, it is an on-going life-long process. <u>It is not just a one time shot</u> and now that you have created a positive level of self-esteem you can stop working at it.

Esteem is like a lot of areas for improvement in this book. <u>They are easy to do</u>. The key to remember is that they are also easy not to do. There is nothing in this book that is not easy to do with a little commitment, is there? However, it is also easy not to do. Success takes commitment. Let me say it again. Make sales you hobby and career. Study and learn and enjoy your relationships with your customers. As you look at yourself as a professional, your esteem will grow and so will your enjoyment of your work. Sales is an energy business. It takes a high level of physical and mental energy to reach peak performance and handle the deadlines required. As you will come to know, most of the time sales is very rewarding.

CHAPTER 10
SETTING AND ACHIEVING
YOUR GOALS

You might be wondering why we're covering the topic of goal setting in this book on selling. First, we want you to learn to set sales goals. However, goal setting is a vital skill to use in all areas of your life. One of the major points of all of my teaching is the importance of having balance in your life. You won't be successful in sales for long if your personal life is unsuccessful. Eventually, it will wear you down and begin to show in your attitude, thus in your sales abilities. The same applies for the spiritual, emotional and physical aspects of your life. Balance is the key to overall success in your sales career.

What Makes Your Desire Burn

Before we talk about how to choose your goals, it is important that you realize how invaluable goals are to your productivity as a salesperson. Goals are what keep you going when sheer determination cannot. Goals are what the professionals focus on when the daily rigors of selling become somewhat tedious or routine. Goals are your pay-off for all your persistence and hard work. If your goals are not strong and clear pictures in your mind, it will become impossible for you to stand firm against the rejection and demands made by an active selling career.

When you reach one goal, it is important that you immediately set another. Tomorrow's goals keep you focused on today's work. The important thing is to be emotionally involved and connected with your goals. They must be your heart-felt desires. When they are, you will sell from the heart too.

Blueprinting Your Success

You would not consider building anything of importance without some idea of what you wanted as the result, would you? The drawing or sketch you create is called a blueprint. No matter how rough it is, it lets your mind visualize what you want. Your mind can then go to work developing the final plan while you get the project under way. This is the only way the picture can become a reality.

Remember, a house is built one brick or board at a time. Your life is built the same way. If you don't have a blueprint for building and you add a brick or board at random, your building would never become anything more than a disarray of brick and wood. This wouldn't provide you with much satisfaction, would it? How many unhappy people do you know whose lives look like that?

It's a fact that only five percent of the people in the greatest country in the world wind up their working days and retire financially able to take care of themselves. Ninety-five percent of the people in the United States do not plan their lives. They merely accept what happens to them from day to day.

The final product from any plan is most often better than the first drawing because the vast creative power of the mind pulls in all the facts and improves upon them. The part of the mind that does this is called the subconscious. It is, without a doubt, the greatest power on the face of the earth. Not only is it the thing that separates man from animal, it is also the very foundation of our creative abilities. Its power is practically limitless. There are many fantastic and informative books about the power of this great tool that we all possess. Since you have this great tool at your disposal, you may as well learn to use it.

This may come as a shock to you, but you are totally responsible for yourself. In fact, you are the only person who has ever denied you anything. It will get you nowhere to blame anyone else.

Fantastic achievements are within your reach if you will only write them down and make your plan. To reach for success, you must learn not to fear failure. Success and failure walk hand in hand, just inches apart. When you chart your own course, you start to lose your fear. You can then take that first step across the moat of failure unconcerned about what lies below because you have your sights set on a star!

You must understand, though, that many people would like to see you fail because they are afraid to step out and seek new ventures for themselves. Being the good buddies that they are, they want you to continue to be like them. That way they can rationalize their own lack of success. They'll tell others something like this, "What's wrong with my life. John is just like me and he's satisfied." When you tell them of your bigger plans for life, they may say, "What if you fail?" To that we say, "What if you succeed?" It takes a big person to be happy over someone else's success. Big people are usually those who have charted a course in their lives and can relate to your excitement. Find people like that and start investing your time with them rather than your old 'stay-the-same' buddies.

If you haven't yet thought about your future success, we strongly recommend that you do it now! How do you picture yourself now? How do you picture yourself in six months or six years? Without a clear picture of what you want to be, your subconscious mind can't help you get anywhere. You're like a ship without a rudder. You float and are blown around by chance winds and storms. No one knows where your destination will be, least of all you.

You can arrive at many ports in life. Some are bad, many are average and very few are excellent. The odds of <u>drifting</u> into an excellent port are extremely unlikely. Please don't spend your life being a part of someone else's goals. Ninety-five percent of the world does that already.

Put it in Writing!

The human mind is a goal-seeking device. It wants to work toward giving you what you want, but first, you must give it a clear picture of exactly what that is.

Don't be hesitant to write down the descriptions in great detail. Yes, it is time consuming, but don't forget what we talked about in our Time

Management chapter--the importance of taking time to plan time. The same holds true when planning your goals. You have to take the time to plan your future.

Think about it this way. If you never take the time to go through the step-by-step process that we will be doing in this chapter, you will never be clearly directed. How can you recognize and reward your achievements, if you are not clear on what you want to achieve in the first place? While it's true you will not have to worry about failure to achieve your goals if you never bother to set them, you will also never feel the exhilarating satisfaction of seeing your goals become reality. So, let's get busy and write. If you are worrying about the amount of time this chapter will take, then you need to complete it when you can set those worries aside and devote an uninterrupted hour or so. You owe it to yourself to put your plan in motion, so don't delay too long. Until you write down your dreams, they remain just that--dreams. If you are to have a chance at making those dreams a reality, you have to write them down and keep them visible. Now take about another 10-15 minutes to write down, in detailed description, what you have been picturing in your mind as your life 20 years into the future. What kind of person will you be? Where will you live? What will you own? Describe your lifestyle. Include social, family, personal and business aspects.

Not only is it beneficial to write down your goals, but you should keep them in a place where you can look at them often. There is some truth to the statement "Out of sight, out of mind." To avoid losing track of what your goals are, keep them within easy reach.

Writing down goals also helps to make them more real. If you simply think about what you want to have happen, it is too easy to forget the specifics and lose focus. However, if you write down specific goals, you have something concrete to refer to.

It's also great to make a practice of recording your achievements. What a motivator! Here are a couple of suggestions that will help you to see where you began your goal setting, and where you will be going with it in the future. Yes, it is time consuming, but when you get into the habit of doing these things you will recognize their benefits.

How to Turn Your Dreams Into Goals

You will probably have some descriptions that you find impossible to believe in at this point in your life. If you can't believe in a dream, you won't take the steps necessary to make it a reality. Before you just throw those dreams out, ask yourself if they can be altered or modified slightly to be made believable. If you can change them to make them believable, do that. If not, just set them aside for now. Who knows, maybe a few years down the road when you have accomplished another goal you thought difficult, these dreams may seem quite attainable. Don't throw them away, file them in your dream drawer.

By now your list should be looking a bit more realistic. Is it? Good. Look at your descriptions. Are they specific? The danger in responding too generally is that you will not be able to zero in on a specific goal from a vague response. That's what we will be doing later on in the chapter. We will ZERO IN on a specific 20 year goal. For now it is enough that you have a modified, realistic, believable picture of yourself 20 years into the future. Keep your descriptions nearby. We will be referring to them later.

SETTING YOUR GOALS

Now that you have laid the groundwork of picturing some dreams and the possibility of turning those dreams into reality, let's talk about other things to keep in mind before the actual goal setting gets under way. While it is productive to set goals for your career, it is just as important to have goals that are personal. It's called having balance in your life. Having a balanced life requires the achievement of balanced goals.

Balance Your Goals

As you first practice setting your goals, it may help you to separate them into categories so you will be better able to keep a balanced life. Listed below are the five suggested categories:

1. Business

This is a given. Most of you are already thinking along the lines of increasing your incomes and improving your sales skills and techniques.

But it doesn't end here. If you have chosen sales as your profession, there are two ways to grow and prosper in it. First of all, make selling your hobby and, secondly, fall in love with the sales business as your chosen career.

2. Personal

It is necessary to take time out for self-improvement. We have talked about keeping yourself physically and mentally fit, and there is no better way to assure this will be done than by setting goals and working toward their achievement. This is probably one of the most neglected areas in the lives of most busy salespeople. Are you seeing where the balance is coming in?

3. Family

This is also one of those areas that is frequently left to take care of itself. Plan family goals. Make your time with your family quality time, not just time that you spend in the same room with them. Plan social events that everyone will enjoy.

4. Spiritual

When I first started training in the field of sales and manage-ment over 20 years ago, I burned with primarily one desire -- to teach people who had chosen sales and entrepreneurial activities as careers the seven fundamentals of selling. The result of this has been that many of my students have earned very high incomes.

Today, my direction is somewhat changed because I am finding totally fulfilled people are not just striving to make a successful living. They are striving to live successfully. Your spiritual growth is a very personal decision. Often it is based on your upbringing, and on people who come into your life that impress you with their beliefs and have answers to the questions you ask about life. You owe it to yourself to continually search and study.

Here's what happened to me when I began my search for spiritual fulfillment. Quite a few years ago, I was introduced to a business leader who represented Dr. Bill Bright of Life 2000 in Arrowhead Springs, California.

He shared with me four spiritual laws that enabled me to have a personal relationship with God through His Son, Jesus Christ. It has made a tremendous difference in my life. I share this with you not to impress my beliefs upon you, but just to let you know where I am coming from at this point in my growth.

5. Recreational

These should be a combination of fun for you alone and times with your family. But, it should **not** be coupled with business. You need time to bust loose, let down your hair. If business opportunities come your way during this time, that's great, however, don't let them interfere with your fun. This is the "take time to smell the roses" time.

6. Emotional

As human beings, we will experience highs and lows in all areas of our lives. Life seems to be a combination of happy and sad, good fortune and crisis. It is imperative that we strive to become emotionally stable people. That, to me, means the events that happen in our lives don't dictate our attitudes and feelings. In essence, I believe we should be happy most of the time.

7. Intellectual

By intellectual, I mean keeping your mind active. Learn new things. Develop new interests. Grow. It doesn't matter whether your interests lie in music, art, investment and finance or gardening. The mental processes used in satisfying your curiosity about a topic will keep you sharp.

An important thing to keep in mind when setting balanced goals is to involve others in the process when necessary. For example, if you are planning your family goals, ask your spouse and children to contribute. After all, they will be contributing to the achievement of these goals, so they should have some say-so in their development. If it is business goals you are setting, and they involve the participation of peers or support staff in your office, let them help you.

There is a two-fold benefit to your goal planning when others are involved. First, you will be surprised how involving others will help to keep you on track. When others benefit from the achievement of your goals, they will make sure you are taking the necessary steps to achieve them. This happens in business as well as in your personal life.

Second, when your business associates and support staff feel a part of, and a sense of responsibility for the future success of the company, they will usually work much harder to assure you meet your goals. As you involve others in your goal setting process, be sure to involve them in the rewards you will receive when those goals are achieved. Who knows, you may spur others to begin setting goals for themselves. It's amazing how contagious success can be.

Make a Binding Contract With Yourself

The following is an example of a contract I suggest you use with every goal you set. By now, you should have noted that I used the word "contract" here -- one of the words I've asked you never to use with customers. I purposefully used that term here because I want you to understand the gravity you need to put on goal setting. Without goals, we are little more than feathers in the wind, drifting wherever the air currents take us. I drafted this agreement with all the seriousness of a legal business agreement because that's how serious I am about my goals. I won't put anything in writing on these sheets until I am certain the goal is something I am willing to work hard to obtain. I don't want goals to be as easily changed as appointments. Without serious, committed goals, humans procrastinate, stagnate and live ultimately unsatisfied lives. Please read this agreement in a businesslike manner and be serious about goal setting. It can take you as far as you desire to go.

(See following page)

PROPOSAL and AGREEMENT
Binding Contract of Commitment with the
"Person in the Mirror"

_____19_____

Name_____

The undersigned proposes to furnish all materials and perform all labor necessary to complete the following goal:

_____
_____
_____
_____
_____
_____
_____
_____

I hereby swear to start today to reach out and do more with my life and achieve the greatness that I know lies within me, which is waiting to be brought out.

From this day forward I will not be denied any longer. This is a day in my life that I finally get the guts to do what I know must be done and quit taking the easy way out, I will pay the price that is necessary to reach this goal because I know the pain of not fulfilling myself is greater than the pain of doing any job no matter how hard.

I understand that my life's plan is going to be reached by reaching one goal at a time, each being but one step toward my greater future. I understand that each contract I fulfill always puts me one step closer to what I want out of life, and I will not have to settle for what others give me or just earn a living. I have a power to change my life.

_____

Signature of Commitment

As I OK this contract, I understand that my future is in my hands only and I can look to no one else for its fulfillment.

ACCEPTANCE

I, as agent for the face in the mirror, upon the completion of this goal congratulate you for proving once again that you can do anything that you want and be anything that you want. You can also get anything that you want as long as you know what it is.

You have taken one more step toward being the person you dream of. You may take great pride in knowing that you have the backbone to plan and reach a goal.

You are now one step closer to your major goal. As you know, major goals are just a string of successful small goals that lead you to the top.

_____

Agent for the "Face in the Mirror"

Date Goal Fulfilled _____19_____

TERMS AND CONDITIONS

1.   Use this contract with yourself for any goal, no matter how small or large. A goal, no matter how small, should be treated with great respect because it builds your character and self image.

2.   Must be filled out in full and dated with starting and completion dates.

3.   Your goal should be very descriptive and explicit. It should paint a very clear picture of what is wanted and when.

4.   All of your contracts that have not been completed, should be read in front of the mirror every day with great conviction, so as to imbed your goals into your subconscious mind.

5.   When a goal is reached, sign as agent for "The Face in the Mirror" and then write in large red letters on the face of the contract, "This contract fulfilled." Save all of these contracts and keep them in order by date completed, so as to see a growth pattern. You will be able to draw great strength from this string of success that you have accomplished, no matter how small they may seem at first.

6.   Remember, you can be as great as anyone, but you must have a plan. Each of these goals, no matter how small, will become a part of that plan and help you to turn your beautiful dreams into a fantastic, rewarding life.

7.   Do not make conflicting goals such as: I will spend more time at home and I will double my sales. These goals may not work together and may cause frustration in your life.

8.   Your goals should be something you want bad enough to turn you on and light your soul on fire and make you move and act with enthusiasm.

9.   What you are doing is deadly serious. You cannot reach a place that you want to go if you do not know how to get there. It is the same way with life. Each one of these goals become a stopping point or starting point on the road map of your life. They will become the blueprint for your every success. If you don't have a blueprint, how are you going to build your life?

      Please, take these extremely seriously no matter how small each goal. Reward yourself and congratulate yourself for starting the habit of planning your life. You will reap unbelievable rewards.

10-100 If you want your life to change, you have to change or you are going to stay just about the same as you are. So set some goals that turn you on and get your life into gear. You can do it -- You can change and become or do anything you want. *Just want!*

Keep all fulfilled contracts in a binder or folder, filed by date. It's fascinating to look back on them a few years down the road. It's also extremely motivating when you see the pile of completed goals building and have a series of successes to look back on.

Success Journals

When you have done an exceptional job in achieving a goal, perhaps even going beyond what you hoped for, it is a good idea to record these "highs" in a journal. Not every achievement will fall into this exceptional category, but those that do deserve to be looked back on and remembered. As you write down the descriptions of your achievements, be sure to be specific. Write down just what an outstanding job you did and how you felt when you achieved your goal. How others may have congratulated you. How you plan to let this achievement give you the momentum to carry you to an even greater achievement. How you plan to reward yourself for a job well done.

Be sure to write in your journal as quickly after achieving your goal as you can. It is at this time that you will have the most excitement and enthusiasm, and these emotions will be important to capture on paper for future motivation. Be very emotional in your writing. Write as if no one will ever see it but yourself. You can even be smug and brag on yourself. It's okay to be a little puffed up with pride in your accomplishments. When you re-read these success stories, you will relive the positive experiences of success you felt. Take advantage of that momentum to get yourself moving in a positive direction on your next goal.

Pep-Talk Tapes

We have already spoken of the benefits of continuing your training by listening to professional sales seminars on video cassettes, but sometimes you need to give yourself a little pep talk about staying on course to achieve the goals you've set. Champions have used this tool and can testify to its effectiveness. Those close to Aristotle Onassis said that he could be found many an evening walking the deck of his luxury liner talking to himself. At times he would talk calmly and sometimes he would tell himself in no uncertain terms what he needed to do.

So use tapes to record different messages to yourself. It is a good idea to make several, depending on what advice you may need at that particular moment. If you need to be encouraged, remind yourself of your accomplishments. Describe some of your best achievements by drawing a detailed picture with your words. At times you can even use your sense of humor to make yourself laugh. There may also be times you need to tell yourself to stop all the complaining and moaning about what isn't going well and start to focus on the positive. You know, the old "pull yourself up by the bootstraps" speech. <u>Sometimes we are our own best teachers</u>.

The recorded tapes can be another method to keep account of your accomplishments. If you don't like the journal method, keep them on tape. Record your excitement and enthusiasm over the consummation of that especially hard to get sale. Have a private conversation with yourself. Listen to the tapes on a day when you are having a very difficult time getting motivated. You will hear the excitement in your voice and the enthusiasm will let you remember how great it was to feel the rewards of all your hard work. Even though you are recording it instead of writing it, remember to give all the details. You will enjoy experiencing your success all over again. This is your chance to be a recording star. Well, maybe not. But it is a chance for you to continue meeting your goals.

Step-By-Step Goal Planning

Until now, you have only dreamed about your future. Yes, you have written your goals down, but they are still in the future. Now you have to turn them into specific goals. There is a step-by-step process to follow to help you to plan and achieve your goals.

You have some idea of what your dreams are 20 years from now, so get your sheet of paper and take another look. Which ones are most important for you to achieve? This is called prioritizing. So rank them in order of importance. Now, how can you make that dream picture come true? The reason I had you be so descriptive is because you can't focus on the entire picture, and **focus** is the key word here. Each detail of your 20 year plan can be a different goal. For example, if your description is more personal, such as, details of how you look physically, write 'personal goal' beside it. However, if your description was a reflection of your financial achievements, you may want to write 'financial goal' beside it.

Go through each of your responses and determine what category each goal fits. When you are finished, be sure that you have at least one response for each aspect of your life that's important so your 20 year plan will be balanced. Upon completion you should have five major 20 year goals. Be sure to be specific in your wording.

Let me illustrate what I mean about being specific in the wording of your goals. Remember, if you are not specific you may not be clear on how to plan your next step. For example, let's pretend your descriptive response to number one went like this:

Example:

"I am the kind of person who spends a lot of time outdoors sailing and swimming. I am slim, healthy, and enjoy the challenge of being the captain of my own sailboat. I am very happy and relaxed in this role, but I also like to talk with others about both my own and their successful careers."

Goal Category

Looking at this description, have I been specific? I have been somewhat specific, but could ZERO IN (remember I said we would be talking more about this) on more details. For example, instead of saying I spend a lot of time outdoors sailing and swimming, I could have said, "I am the kind of person who spends at least three months every year sailing and swimming off the coast of Southern California." Now do you see what I mean by specific? Let's continue to ZERO IN on this description. Instead of saying slim, I could mention exactly what I want to weigh 20 years from now. Instead of saying sailboat, I could say a 32 foot, teak trimmed, double-masted sailboat, named the "Lucy Anne." Instead of talking in vague terms of others around me, I could name those individuals I will be doing business with 20 years from now, or at least describe the type of Champions I have in mind. Now, that is specific, wouldn't you agree?

Now that we have gone back and made the description more specific, we need to pick one of the goal categories to put the description in. Since this description could fit into several categories, it is important to choose the one most important. If the item most important to you is having a 32 foot sailboat, then you might say it would best fit the financial category, because you will need to set proper financial goals in order to afford your sailboat. Or, if being slim and healthy is your main focus, then you would want this to be a personal goal. Then you would take the steps to achieve physical fitness 20 years from now. Do you see what I mean?

Now go through each one of your responses and do exactly as we have done with this one. First make them specific. Then categorize them. When you have completed this exercise, you should have five major well-balanced long-term goals. You have now completed the first step of the goal planning process.

Medium Range Goal Planning

Your 20 year goals are now in place, but those seem so far away you may be asking yourself, "How can I possibly stay focused on goals that will not be achieved for 20 years?" To put things into perspective, if you are old enough, look back 20 years. Isn't it amazing how short a time it seems? Now is 20 years really that far in the future? Of course, if those 20 year goals were the only goals you planned for yourself, you would be looking at an almost impossible task. This is where your step-by-step planning comes into play. Now that you have planned your long range goals, it is time to take the second step and plan your medium range goals.

Since this is medium range goal planning, let's just split that 20 years in half. Where will you need to be 10 years from now to be on track to achieve your 20 year goals? Let's go back to the 20 year goal of having that 32 foot teak trimmed sailboat. First, I need to figure out just how much money it will take to buy this sailboat. Let's say it will cost $50,000 to buy the sailboat of my dreams. Of course, this doesn't take into consideration how much it will cost to dock it, and to invest my free time learning to sail. This is how specific you need to be with your medium range goals. If they are financial, you must discover the major cost and all the possible hidden costs in achieving your goal.

Now, let's pretend my current annual income is $60,000. How much of this $60,000 do I now contribute toward recreation? How much more would I need to make in order to own, maintain, and enjoy my sailboat? All these questions are important in order to properly plan medium range goals.

The thing to remember about goals is they are not written in blood never to be changed or altered. Remember, you are planning 20 years in your future. Much can happen in 20 years, even ten years to change your ideas about where you want to be in the future, so be flexible. Thinking positively, you may be so successful in ten years, that what you planned for your 20 year goals have become obsolete. You sure wouldn't mind being flexible for that, would you?

If you are quite young and reading this book, first of all good for you to get such a head start. I understand that ten years seems like an incredibly long range plan for you. After all, 20 years could be almost as long as you have been around. Don't worry, just do the best you can, but still plan for the 20 years. The thing with youth is you are usually better able to dream.

Not bad, now you have your long and medium range goals planned and are ready to move to the next step--short term goals.

Short Term Goals

These goals can range anywhere from 1-5 years down the road. It should be evident to you by now what you will need to do to achieve your medium range goals, so just keep breaking it down into a step-by-step process. It is especially important that you keep the short term goals within easy reach. These are goals that you will need to look at fairly often when setting and achieving your immediate or daily goals.

Your short term goals are probably not going to be as flexible as your medium and long range goals. As you get past the first year and well into the second, you may have to re-establish new short term goals, but for the most part, these will remain the most constant of the goals you plan. It stands to reason what you plan for just a few years down the road is much more likely to be accurate than what you plan for 20 years into the future.

Immediate Or Daily Goals

These are the goals you have in front of you each day. These are the last steps in planning your goals, but certainly not the least important.

Because it is difficult and often unproductive to focus on more than one thing at a time, it will be vital for you to set these daily goals and focus on their achievement. If you do not write down your daily goals, you have little hope of achieving your 20 year goals.

Let's call your daily goals your "List of Six." There are several ways to go about planning and writing down your daily list of six things you want to accomplish, so you must determine which method will work best for you.

When you are planning your List of Six, plan at a time of day when you have some privacy and time to prepare. In other words, don't begin writing what you want to achieve Wednesday on Wednesday morning at 8:00. It's too late. Champions begin their days long before 8:00, so if your goal is to become a Champion, you must do the most productive thing possible with each hour of your day.

As we covered in our chapter on time planning, if you know that your Wednesday will begin at 6:00 a.m., plan for it the previous day. I like to plan for my Wednesday List of Six, on Tuesday night after I have already achieved my goals for Tuesday. Then, I know exactly what needs to be accomplished for Wednesday, and I have that successful momentum to encourage me to reach just a little further on Wednesday.

It is important that your List of Six be well-balanced to achieve all five of your major long range goals. So each night when you are writing your List of Six, remember to include all the goal categories of (a) business, (b) personal, (c) family, (d) spiritual, and (e) recreation. If you don't set goals to cover all categories, you may cause yourself much unhappiness.

For example, if you meet all your goals in your personal and business categories, but fail to meet those in your family category, you may find yourself isolated from those you love. If you lose contact with the ones you love, whom will you have to share the wonderful rewards you will receive when you achieve your goals? So BE BALANCED!

Set a Time Limit for Goal Achievement

It is only reasonable to think that if you have had to be so specific with your goals, you would need to be just as specific in setting time limits for achieving those goals. So figure out precisely what time you want your 20 year goals to be achieved. Name the year, month and day. Do the same with your medium range and short term goals. Your daily goals are a different matter.

When making your List of Six, you might find it helpful to put them in your Day-Timer® by times in the day you plan to have them accomplished. It is also helpful to list whom you will need to meet or what phone calls you will need to make to achieve each goal. For example, if one of your daily goals is to consummate one sale, you will need to write the names of at least 5-10 hot prospects you will call to make that a possibility. If your daily goal is to go to the gym and work out for at least one hour, you may have to make yourself a note to call your family and let them know you'll be late to dinner. If your daily goal is to reorganize the office, is there anyone else you need to involve?

Set activity goals not just production goals. How many people will you see today? How many presentations will you give? If all your goals are production goals, you're setting yourself up for failure and this will lead to discouragement. Be active. Set activity goals and you'll keep meeting them even during problem periods.

You are probably seeing the need to carry that Day-Timer with you always now, aren't you? Setting goals is an intricate part of creating success for you and those around you who are involved in your goals, so don't just depend on your memory. Take whatever steps are necessary for your success, but act in a timely manner. You can't do this if you have not set definite times for each particular goal to be completed.

Step-By-Step Reinforcement and Rewards

Most salespeople just think of the end reward to achieving their goal, but it can be beneficial to break your rewards into steps just like you did your goals. The more time it takes to achieve your result or goal, the more necessary it is to set up a step-by-step reward system. Make sure that the rewards are proportionate to the accomplishment.

For example, let's say that you have a goal to lose 20 pounds in two months. You have broken your goal into steps, so you know that you will need to lose five pounds a week to achieve your two month goal. Because it is easier to look at the five pound weight loss each week, you decide to make that a daily focus for this goal and set your sights on what it will take on a daily basis to achieve your weekly goal. Now you have your daily goal of losing 3/4 of a pound.

Let's just say for you to lose your required 3/4 pound each day, you will need to consume no more than 1000 calories a day. What you must decide is whether you need a daily reward, or if a weekly reward will suffice. If you are not sure which would be better for you, then try the weekly reward system first. You may decide to buy yourself a new belt when you accomplish your first week goal of losing five pounds.

You first week has gone by, but you lost only four pounds. This could be an indication that you need more motivation. You need more frequent rewards to achieve your goal. You may be asking, "How can I afford to achieve my goals if I have to spend a lot of money on the step-by-step process?" It isn't necessary for your rewards to always involve a financial commitment. You might congratulate yourself each day that you lose 3/4 of a pound. Or, you might ask your spouse to help you meet your goal and offer some verbal reinforcement.

Here is where your creativity can make or break you. You must get very creative with your reinforcements or rewards when you accomplish your goals. They are your motivation to succeed. Don't let lack of proper and frequent rewards inhibit your achievements. When I write, and accomplish what I needed to for that day's work, I might allow myself a walk, or a thirty minute private time listening to my favorite music. Those things don't really require a financial commitment, unless of course you count time as money, and that I do. But, I give this to myself as a reward. Remember, your rewards must be in proportion to your achievements. It will be very anti-climactic if you accomplish a difficult goal only to have no "pot at the end of the rainbow." Don't make yourself work for nothing.

Celebrate Your Achievements

Even though this is a part of the reinforcement for accomplishing your goals, some people don't know how to do this with a bang. When you come toward the end of a long project, let your enthusiasm build for the final accomplishment of your goal. The longer you plan and focus on achieving that goal, the more celebration there should be at its end.

This is not the time to be modest. Give yourself a time to bask in the enjoyment of the moment. By doing this you will be ready to begin your next project with verve and enthusiasm. You will feel renewed both phys- ically and mentally and ready to tackle tomorrow's goals. The more fun you have when you accomplish a goal, the more you want to repeat the performance. Think about it, in order to repeat the celebration, you have to achieve another difficult goal. Can you feel the momentum? Don't for- get to record your exceptional successes. It may even be fun to video record your celebration. Then you could simply pop the video into the VCR and relive the excitement. Talk about motivation! Goals are said to be the "engine of achievement." If goals are the engine of achievement, then the celebration is really letting off the steam!

Leaving Your Comfort Zone

This is one of the hardest things to do--leave your comfort zone. This is the biggest reason many salespeople leave what could be a financially and emotionally rewarding career for them. They just can't stand to be out of their comfort zone. Leaving your comfort zone is not only hard for the new salesperson, it is especially hard to do if you are already moder- ately successful in sales and decide to do more. It is so tempting to just sit back, relax, and let the good times roll.

Champions face leaving their comfort zone on a daily basis. They feel fear and discomfort just like the average salesperson, but they have learned to get tough with themselves. They have learned through experi- ence the value of putting themselves outside their comfort zones. Isn't that where all the growth is? Take a look at what causes discomfort -- a growing or learning experience. You won't find much to stimulate your growth inside your comfort zone. When we repeatedly make ourselves do things we don't normally do, those things soon become familiar and lose their fear factor. If you don't give yourself a chance to be friends with the unfamiliar, you will never learn new skills.

Ask yourself this, is being comfortable most important to me? You would be surprised at how many salespeople would answer "yes" to that question. It must go back to being in the womb with your built-in pool, your automatic chauffeur and maid, and all the food you could ask for. What service! But, wouldn't it get lonely and boring if that's what you had to look forward to all day? I say, if everyone were merely comfort-able, they would be easily bored and discontent with life. Have you ever looked forward to taking a relaxing vacation only to discover after the third day you are bored with the routine of it all? Champion salespeople are excited and challenged by the job of selling. They get used to living on the edge, so to them, comfort isn't all it's cracked up to be.

I'm not talking about making yourself so uncomfortable you are unable to function. I'm talking about not allowing yourself to postpone your success because you have to face a little fear and discomfort. The discomfort is very short lived. Look at it as an adventure. The more you do it, the more you put yourself on that edge, the more you'll like feeling the excitement of achieving what others call the impossible.

Typical Reasons for Failure to Accomplish Goals

It would be terrific if we could all achieve our goals 100% of the time, but this is unrealistic thinking. As much as I want you to be positive thinkers, I want you to be successful in the process. So, I have listed some common problems that contribute to failure to accomplish goals.

1. Setting Unrealistic Goals

If you do not determine what is reachable for you to begin with, you have set yourself up for failure. That is the value of the step-by-step method of setting and achieving goals. It is a monitoring system. If you have worked hard and are still unable to reach your goal, perhaps you have set what is for now an unreachable goal. Don't scrap the goal alto-gether, modify it. Break it down into smaller, more do-able pieces.

2. Haven't Taken Ownership of the Goals

By not taking ownership of your goals, I mean you haven't set g o a l s that are your own to begin with. You may be working with goals that your company wants, or your family wants, but until you want your goals, you won't do much toward achieving them.

3. Lack of Focus

This problem usually indicates a breakdown in the step-by-step process. For example, if you set your short term goals, but have not been able to reach them, you probably are having a problem with your daily or immediate goal setting. You will have to go back to the smallest step. Did you write down your List of Six? It's like a snowball affect. When you achieve one goal it gives you the momentum to continue toward achieving the next, each one getting bigger and bigger.

4. Failure to Be Specific

You may not be achieving your goals because you failed to make them specific enough and to set deadlines for your achievement. Too general goal setting means too little direction toward achievement.

5. Inaccurate or Infrequent Reward System

We spoke about this earlier. If you do not reward yourself often enough or well enough you will not see the value in accomplishing your goals. There is hardly a one of us that likes to work for nothing. You lose all the excitement and enthusiasm for doing the job if you go a long time with no reward. Be good to yourself.

6. Poor Self-Image

In Chapter 9, I spoke about the importance of having a positive outlook and high level of self-esteem. If you do not believe you are capable of achieving your goals, you won't be. If you realize that believing in yourself is a problem, you may want to re-read Chapter 9. Don't let a poor perspective hold you back from all the wonderful things awaiting you in your selling career.

7. Conflicting Goals

We talked about this earlier in the goals contract. I would like to stress again how frustrated you can become if you set goals that conflict. Make sure you have harmony and balance when setting your goals.

Expect Good Things to Happen

Don't rely on having good luck, expect it. Professionals don't expect trouble, they plan ways to prevent it. I hope you will study, re-read, and commit yourself to using the information in this chapter. People who are successful plan their goals to be successful.

As I've said over and over, you must keep balance in your professional and personal life. Plan and take the time to be with your family, to enjoy your children, to enjoy your success. Don't be so caught up in making a living that you forget to make a life. Material things will come and go in your life, the people in your life are what's really important. Don't forget to do these things:

1. Plan what you want.
2. Plan how you will get it.
3. Plan to live a balanced life.
4. Plan to continue your life-long journey of education.
5. Plan to seek out new opportunities.
6. Plan the best use of your time.
7. Plan to help others along the way.

We have invested a lot of time on goals, but I feel it is what drives sales, both short term and long term. The selling business requires a lot of energy and goals are the fuel for that energy. If we don't know why we are working or what we are working for, we will find it extremely difficult to stay the course. Don't set yourself up for disappointments by not having a clear vision of what your target or goal is. In spite of all that has been written on goals, not more than 20% of our population have written goals or plan for their lives beyond their next vacation. Start today. You will feel and see a big difference in your attitude about each and every customer contact. As my associate and fellow educator, Jim Rohn says, "It's easy to do and easy not to do."

CHAPTER 11
ADDITIONAL METHODS, TECHNIQUES, AND STEPS FOR SALES SUCCESS

Definition of Success

Before we go any further, let me introduce you to what I mean by success. Imprint these words upon your memory. The definition of success I would ask you to remember is this:

Success is the continuous journey
toward the achievement of predetermined, worthwhile goals.

There is no arriving at success once you totally comprehend what it is. Because we are continually growing and changing as individuals, and the world around us is changing, the achievement of success has to be a continuing process.

Let's say you decide that you'll be a success when you earn $50,000 per year. $50,000 per year might be a great goal for you now, but once you achieve it and get used to it, you'll set your sights on something bigger and better. It's normal. Most of us will always want more. Very few people ever reach a point in their lives where they are completely satisfied and content, willing to stay just like they are for the rest of their lives.

Pre-determined means we have written a plan. We have a blueprint for our success. We have chosen ourselves a set course rather than letting our reaction to the world determine what our lives will be like.

Worthwhile is a very important word in our definition, too. This means that you believe you can achieve success. That you burn with the desire to achieve it and you have increased your emotional ability to handle it when you get it. If you work to achieve a goal you want but don't truly believe you are worthy of, you can ruin your life. You can lose friends, your job, your family. So, it's essential when you set your goals that you are confident that you are worthy of whatever your consider success to be.

Now that you understand the concept of sales success being a constant journey, and you have accepted the need to feel satisfaction and happiness on this journey, I would like you to internalize a more personal meaning of what selling should mean to you. In order to be a true professional, you need to do more than just accept selling as your chosen career. It has to go deeper than that.

We have talked extensively about appealing to your customer's emotional needs, and also about the importance of analyzing your own needs. To the great Champions, **selling is a hobby they love, and they are committed to devoting many hours of research, study, and practice to its development**.

Look at this definition again. What does this require you to do? Nothing less than to **fall in love with selling**. Oh sure, many average people in sales have chosen this career because they can be their own boss, or because they can take those two hour extended lunches without being called on the carpet about it. They even dream about all the perks and special benefits that the professionals get. So why don't those benefits apply to the average salesperson's career? **It's because they are not in love with selling. They are not willing to do what they know they should do to be successful.**

I would like to emphasize how important selling is to professionals. It is all consuming. Their methods and techniques become so ingrained and automatic, they practice them in all aspects of their lives. After all, when you have such tremendous success in business, wouldn't you want that for your personal life too? For example, when you have seen the powerful results of using the quiet approach introduced in this book, the most natural thing to do would be to practice it in your personal relationships with family and friends, and see how much more rewarding they become.

Personal Costs of Being a Professional

If we are to look at a professional career in sales realistically, we must realize it comes with a cost. I'm sure you have all heard the saying, "You get what you pay for." Well, this is true with earning your way to Championship sales. If you see those professionals enjoying the benefits of a successful career and you want those same privileges, what is holding you back? Don't you believe you deserve them? Or is it you don't want to pay the price? The ironic thing is, if you are not now living up to your sales potential, you are already paying the price. You are caught in a web of fear, procrastination, and deferred dreams. Wouldn't you agree that's too high a price to pay? Even if you are somewhat successful, but could increase your income and personal enjoyment, you are also paying a price.

If you are a professional who has achieved success in the past, but now you find yourself struggling to keep up, where do you go from here? This is a common problem with everyone. How do you know where you went wrong? How do you begin to get back on track? This is where time audits and sales charts come in handy. We talked more about this in Chapter Eight on Self-Management. We included sample charts and time audit forms to assist you in getting back on the road to success. All this takes time, and giving up some of your free time may be the price you pay. I really don't agree with that statement "FREE" time anyway. Hopefully, you did your own time audit as discussed in Chapter Eight and learned just how much your time is worth.

You may be saying, "Tom, I'm willing to pay the price to become a Champion, but I don't know how to take the steps that help me to be successful. I can understand that confusion; I've been there myself. Even though you have read all the previous chapters to help you with specific parts of your preparation, presentation, and consummation of sales, you may be having difficulty pulling it all together. This is where continuous study, practice, drill and rehearsal will help you develop a mature, professional manner, tailor-made for your success.

If you find yourself stumbling over one area, go back and review. If you still can't find your answer, write it down and keep it in a special file of things you wish to research -- then do the research. Because, what is the definition of success? It's a **journey**. It's a constant on-going process that requires a commitment on the part of the traveler.

All the methods and techniques taught in this book will not assist you in your journey if you do not practice, drill, and rehearse them. That's the price. Sales is not something you do as a lark. If you are willing to pay the price of a true Champion, you must **be able to change to relate to the people you must serve. You must adopt the mannerisms of a highly skilled individual. You must be a person of unquestionable integrity and maintain high moral values.** Lastly, you must do all these things with enjoyment and genuine pleasure. With a smile on your face, repeat this line:

I am a top professional. I leave nothing to chance.
I am neat and efficient in every aspect of my career.

Make this your personal, professional mission statement. Living with this as your 'theme' will practically guarantee your success. It will help you keep on track with your lifelong goals, keeping distractions at bay. Until you succeed at fully living your motto, there are many distractions you need to beware of. They can take you far off course. So far, in fact, that it will take concerted effort and time to get back on track.

Distractions on Your Road to Success

1. <u>Success Itself</u>. One of the main distractions on your road to success is, ironically enough, experiencing success itself. Once many salespeople have tasted success and from their hard work have achieved a higher income, a more prestigious position with the company, or enjoyment of certain perks in their personal lives, they may forget what brought them success in the first place.

For example, let's take a look at Ms. Oncewas. She once was a top salesperson with Go Get Them, Inc. She once was first to volunteer to attend the sales training seminars, and constantly returned to the office with a renewed enthusiasm for selling. She once was reluctant to take that extended lunch hour with a friend when she knew she had work to do.

She once was busy checking her daily goals to make sure she stayed on target to meet her long-term goals.

Are you getting the picture? Ms. Oncewas was so influenced by her own success she forgot to continue to make goals and then extend herself to achieve them. She thought her success journey was at its end. What a dangerous position in which to find herself. If you are a true professional salesperson, you will never reach the end of your journey, and it won't even matter because you are doing what you love to do.

2. <u>Procrastination</u>. This great killer of success comes directly after, if not simultaneously with, number one. You begin to put off doing what you know you should do to maintain that professional level of success. You have to guard against procrastination every day. Talk to yourself. Tell yourself you are going to practice, drill, and rehearse. Get yourself pumped up. We talked about this in our Chapter on Goals.

3. <u>Fear</u>. When you see your sales drop, you begin to fear losing the lifestyle to which you have become accustomed. Fear breeds insecurity. All this may have come about because you put your needs before that of your customers. If that was the case, get the dollar signs out of your eyes. Don't act in **need** of a sale. This will put the kiss of death to a potentially successful sale. Go back and analyze what made you successful in the first place, and zero in on what went wrong. You cannot be sincere with your customers until your focus is on them, not yourself.

4. <u>Not Giving Attention to Detail</u>. It can be such a temptation to skip those little things that influenced your success. After all, you are busy and don't have time for them any longer. Please believe me when I say this, in today's market it can often be that attention to detail that separates you from your competition. I can understand not wanting to spend your valuable time with follow-up and service when you could be out there making new contacts, making sales, and most importantly making more money. You owe it to your customers to provide them with as high a quality service as you did when you were asking for their business. If you are asking yourself where you will find the time, you may be surprised what you find if you do a time audit. Hours hidden here and there in

unnecessary interruptions. So, my suggestion for you is to first audit your time before you complain about having no time. If you still don't feel you have the time, look at what needs to be changed, then change it. For example, if you are spending four hours doing yard work, you have to ask yourself if this is the best use of your time. If the answer is no, then hire someone else to do the yard. This will free you up to do the most productive thing with every hour of every day.

5. <u>Poor Judgment</u>. This can be one of the hardest distractions to recognize and control. Your entire attitude can change when you make assumptions about your customers based on your own personal prejudice or experiences. Try to see each new customer with fresh eyes. I have said it before, but it bears repeating, while you are judging your customers, they will be judging you. Whether you realize it or not, when you make assumptions about your customers you wear your feelings on your face and show them through your attitude. If you take a close look at those you are judging, chances are they will be mirroring your expressions and actions. So if you have to judge your customers, make your judgments positive.

6. <u>Fads in Selling</u>. From time to time, people come up with the latest thing in selling that will change your career. These ideas may have fancy names and many of them may make you feel good about what you are doing, but if you don't have a solid foundation of selling skills to build on, none of these new fads will help you for long.

Remember the above six major distractions to building and maintaining a successful sales career. Whenever you let yourself be sidetracked in even one of these areas, you will lose your competitive edge.

Seven Steps in Sales
Take a look again at the seven steps in sales discussed in Chapter One:

1. Prospecting
2. Making Original Contact
3. Qualification
4. Presentation
5. Handling Objections

6. Consummation

7. Getting Referrals

Review this list one more time and answer these questions. Which ones are your strengths? Which ones are your weaknesses? Do you know? If you cannot identify your sales strengths and weaknesses, it is time you found out.

There are several good methods on the market that can help you determine what needs work in your sales career. We market one called the $ales $uccess Profile®. It gives you 50 simple selling situations and multiple choice answers. Your answers help us develop a graph of your strengths and weaknesses in the specific skills required to succeed in selling. The profile also prints out an explanation and tips for improving those particular skills in which you could use some help. I highly recommend anyone whose personal happiness or career success depends on his or her ability to persuade or sell others an idea, concept, product or service, seriously consider completing one of these evaluations for yourself. It asks questions about your personal selling style and gives situations to consider in order to determine your particular abilities. Once you complete the evaluation, it is scored. Your answers help us develop a graph of your strengths and weaknesses in the specific skills required to succeed in selling. The profile also prints out an explanation and tips for improving those particular skills with which you could use some help.

I like to compare the value of a tool such as the $ales $uccess Profile to that of a directory found in a shopping center. Upon entering the mall, we seek out the directory to show us to our desired destination — a particular store or restaurant. We can usually locate where we want to be rather easily on the directory. Tell me, though, just how effective that directory would be if it didn't also include a little red dot or arrow labeled, "You are here"? Not very. The $ales $uccess Profile will provide you with the "You are here" symbol for your personal directory for success in your sales career. It will give you a starting point from which you can take the steps necessary to reach your ultimate career destination.

We have found the $ales $uccess Profile to be an excellent tool for salespeople to learn how to work smarter on their selling skills, not just to work harder at selling. It's also a great addition to your resume, allowing a sales manager to evaluate your abilities in detail before hiring you. I don't know too many sales managers who would pass up the opportunity to interview such a sales candidate.

The sales evaluation is beneficial to the experienced salesperson as well as the novice. Do yourself a favor and evaluate what your true sales strengths and weaknesses are.

Throughout this book, we've recommended several other resources as aids to your continued growth and development. Those products developed by and available from our company are:

1. $ales $uccess Profile - A 50-question sales skill evaluation designed to help you determine your strengths and areas where you could rapidly improve your income. See how you stack up against over 400,000 salespeople that have taken this evaluation.

2. How to Master the Art of Selling hard cover book - The million-selling book on specific "how-to" sales techniques and strategies. This book has launched the careers of millions of sales professionals. (The trade paperback version is available through Warner Books and is carried by most bookstores in the U. S.)

3. Professional Selling from A to Z video program - Our complete nuts and bolts sales training video program. You not only hear the material, you can see the subtleties demonstrated in role play situations. Over 10,000 businesses around the world use Tom Hopkin's video training systems.

4. *Selling Style Personal Video Tape - If a picture is worth a thousand words then this video is certainly worth millions of words. This single video tape includes excerpts of Tom Hopkins demonstrating the low profile style using the selling skills taught in this book. This might be particularly useful to someone who does not already have a successful style and would like to emulate one of the world's top sales professionals as they develop a style of their own.

*Because you have invested in this book, you will receive a 50% discount on our Low Profile Selling Style Personal video tape. See page 232 for details.

5. Guide to Greatness in Sales hard cover book - There's more to the field than the simple act of selling. Learn to avoid a lifetime of career mistakes and open the door to a lifetime of career opportunities.

6. Academy of Master Closing - This audio program was developed to take the sales professional to an advanced level of competence. Learn the secrets top producers (who have mastered the basics) use in their customer contacts.

7. Boot Camp - This 3-day live seminar is unlike any other sales training experience you'll ever encounter. You won't just hear the material and take notes for three solid days.   You will live the material, internalizing it well enough to begin benefiting from it on your very next customer contact.

Tom Hopkins only teaches his rigorous and highly popular Boot Camp selling techniques to the general public on a bi-annual basis. Customized Boot Camp programs for companies and industries can be arranged by contacting Tom Hopkins International.

These highly praised and highly successful retreats have trained over 20,000 salespeople who have boasted up to 100% increase in their selling skills after graduating. The depth of the material covered and the total immersion of the students in the material is quite unlike any other sales training program available. Tom Hopkins' Boot Camp will transform your sales career. It will also put you to the test, so if you don't have what it takes or are not really serious about selling, it's recommended that you don't sign up! Although the training will be grueling and tough, once you've completed it, you'll be armed with the knowledge and confidence to put you on the road to success.

8. Sales Mastery - For those students who prefer individual, personalized sales training, we offer the Sales Mastery Personal Coaching program where you have a personal coach help you learn the basics as they apply to your particular selling situation.

Tom Hopkins International can be reached at 7531 East Second Street, Scottsdale, Arizona 85251. You can also get information by calling 800-528-0446 or (602) 949-0786. Our FAX number is (602) 949-1590. Our customer service representatives will be happy to answer your questions.

We have many other products available as well. You may want to request a free copy of our product catalog.

9. Day-Timer Concepts - For the best in time planning tools, we highly recommend Day-Timer products. They can be reached at:

Day-Timer Concepts
One Day-Timer Plaza
Allentown, Pennsylvania 18195-1551
800-556-5430

Invest in yourself to turn your weaknesses into strengths. Then congratulate yourself on all the hard work that went into developing those strengths. Good! Now take an honest look at your weaknesses. Have you ever taken the time to consider why they are your weaknesses? Chances are you feel good when you know you have employed your strengths, and they have paid off. You have consummated the sale. Because you feel a sense of achievement and reward when exhibiting your strengths, you continue to practice and fine tune them, and not your weaknesses.

If we look at your weaknesses, we will see another scenario, won't we? Nobody likes to do what they are not good at, so the common practice is to avoid dwelling on the weaknesses. Please listen to these next few words, if you commit yourself to making your weaknesses your strengths, you will dramatically increase your sales. In other words, master your weaknesses. Don't let your weaknesses control your sales ratio. Sure it will be uncomfortable at first, perhaps even painful, but soon you will feel the excitement of overcoming a challenge. Don't abandon your dependable sales techniques that have brought you the success you now enjoy. Rather focus on the techniques you have not yet incorporated into your presentation, and begin to practice, drill, and rehearse what makes you feel uncomfortable. Don't distance yourself from your weaknesses; make them your best friends.

Closing Words

If you think it's hard nowadays to be successful in selling, I would respectfully fall back on my 30 years of experience to disagree with you and I will tell you why. Ninety percent of your competition is searching for a quick, easy way to success with lots of short cuts and no fundamentals or learning to test what we know. Most people like to attend seminars that make them feel good, but usually leave with no real content. They also have no time to build a solid foundation of skills and values that will carry them through lean times. We are even paying the price in many of our public schools with no fundamentals. Now the idea seems to be 'just make us feel good and let us out so we can sink to the bottom of the economic ladder'. I can just about guarantee you success if you take exactly the opposite approach--a program of dedicated learning of the fundamentals of selling. I don't mean a half-baked attempt, I mean an apprenticeship of the old days. You will leave your competition in the dust as they swerve down the road looking for more short cuts.

I hope you noticed that I used the word Champion a lot in this book. It's because no one becomes a Champion without hard work and dedication to being the greatest in their field of endeavor. The words short cut, easy, and no fundamentals don't go with the word Champion. I hope you agree. We all know in our hearts whether we are paying the price to be average or a Champion. What does your heart tell you? If you don't like the answer, you have the power to change and it is my fondest wish that this book will help.

INDEX